I0454965

THREATS TO THE AMERICAN HOMELAND AFTER KILLING BIN LADEN: AN ASSESSMENT

HEARING

BEFORE THE

COMMITTEE ON HOMELAND SECURITY

HOUSE OF REPRESENTATIVES

ONE HUNDRED TWELFTH CONGRESS

FIRST SESSION

MAY 25, 2011

Serial No. 112–25

Printed for the use of the Committee on Homeland Security

Available via the World Wide Web: http://www.gpo.gov/fdsys/

U.S. GOVERNMENT PRINTING OFFICE

72–235 PDF   WASHINGTON : 2012

COMMITTEE ON HOMELAND SECURITY

PETER T. KING, New York, *Chairman*

LAMAR SMITH, Texas
DANIEL E. LUNGREN, California
MIKE ROGERS, Alabama
MICHAEL T. MCCAUL, Texas
GUS M. BILIRAKIS, Florida
PAUL C. BROUN, Georgia
CANDICE S. MILLER, Michigan
TIM WALBERG, Michigan
CHIP CRAVAACK, Minnesota
JOE WALSH, Illinois
PATRICK MEEHAN, Pennsylvania
BEN QUAYLE, Arizona
SCOTT RIGELL, Virginia
BILLY LONG, Missouri
JEFF DUNCAN, South Carolina
TOM MARINO, Pennsylvania
BLAKE FARENTHOLD, Texas
MO BROOKS, Alabama

BENNIE G. THOMPSON, Mississippi
LORETTA SANCHEZ, California
SHEILA JACKSON LEE, Texas
HENRY CUELLAR, Texas
YVETTE D. CLARKE, New York
LAURA RICHARDSON, California
DANNY K. DAVIS, Illinois
BRIAN HIGGINS, New York
JACKIE SPEIER, California
CEDRIC L. RICHMOND, Louisiana
HANSEN CLARKE, Michigan
WILLIAM R. KEATING, Massachusetts
VACANCY
VACANCY

MICHAEL J. RUSSELL, *Staff Director/Chief Counsel*
KERRY ANN WATKINS, *Senior Policy Director*
MICHAEL S. TWINCHEK, *Chief Clerk*
I. LANIER AVANT, *Minority Staff Director*

CONTENTS

THREATS TO THE AMERICAN HOMELAND AFTER KILLING BIN LADEN: AN ASSESSMENT

Wednesday, May 25, 2011

U.S. House of Representatives,
Committee on Homeland Security,
Washington, DC.

The committee met, pursuant to call, at 9:33 a.m., in Room 311, Cannon House Office Building, Hon. Peter T. King [Chairman of the committee] presiding.

Present: Representatives King, Smith, Lungren, Rogers, McCaul, Broun, Miller, Walberg, Cravaack, Walsh, Meehan, Rigell, Duncan, Marino, Farenthold, Brooks, Thompson, Jackson Lee, Cuellar, Clarke of New York, Richardson, Davis, Speier, Richmond, Clarke of Michigan and Keating.

Chairman KING. Good morning. The Committee on Homeland Security will come to order.

The committee is meeting today to examine the near-term and long-term consequences and benefits to the security of our homeland resulting from the successful killing of Osama bin Laden. I now recognize myself for an opening statement.

First of all, let me welcome everyone here this morning. Let me especially thank our witnesses. We have an outstanding panel of witnesses, and I truly look forward to their testimony. I want to thank the Ranking Member, as always, for his assistance in this hearing. My remarks will be brief this morning.

I believe this hearing is absolutely essential for a number of reasons. One, all of us can take great satisfaction and pride, quite frankly, in the killing of Osama bin Laden. I give the President tremendous credit for having done it. It took courage. It took basically ice water in his veins at the last moment to make that decision, and I give him tremendous credit for it.

The only concern I have is that too many, I think, of the American people somehow feel that now with bin Laden dead, as great a victory as this was, and we can discuss how great it was, how significant it was, what the implications are, the fact is I believe too many people think that with bin Laden dead, somehow the war against terrorism is over, or the terrorist war against us is over; that this will significantly impact the war against us; and somehow maybe we should step back and let our guard down, maybe we can relax, maybe start cutting back in some of the programs that have kept us safe over the last 10 years.

My own belief is that in the short run, the threat is probably greater than it was. Long term, there is no doubt that the death of bin Laden is extremely positive for so many different reasons.

But in the short run in particular, I think it is very likely to assume—and just looking at al-Qaeda's own language—the fact is that they feel they have to not just avenge this, but they have to show the rest of the world, the rest of the Muslim world, the rest of the terror world, that they are viable, that they are vibrant as before, that they have not been taken down, and they have to have a dramatic showing. That, to me, would involve obviously an attack by al-Qaeda or one of its franchise operations.

My belief is that because of the many programs that have been instituted over the last 9, 10 years, it would be very difficult for al-Qaeda to carry out another 9/11-type attack, attack from overseas into the United States, certainly not on the dimensions of the September 11 attacks. But at the same time, starting several years ago, al-Qaeda did begin recruiting in this country people under the radar screen. In addition to that, we have had those who are self-radicalized, those who are radicalized through the internet. We have seen a series of cases, for instance, just in New York, Najibullah Zazi, the subway bomber, who was totally under the radar screen, who was taken to Afghanistan for training and came back to this country and came within hours of carrying out a massive attack on the New York City subway system.

We had Major Hasan, who was in a way self-radicalized through his dealings with Awlaki over the internet, and what he carried out at Fort Hood in the fall of the 2009. Then we had Shahzad, the Times Square bomber, again, under the radar screen, an American citizen trained by the Pakistani Taliban, who came, again, very close to a successful attack in Times Square.

So with all of this, I look forward to the witnesses telling us exactly what they see both in the long term and the short term, what it means that bin Laden is no longer here, what it means as far as our defenses, where we should be looking to for the next attack, the type of attack it could be, the dimensions of that attack. Also, as far as the power structure in al-Qaeda, who is going to take over? Is there anyone who has the capability of having the type of evil magnetism that bin Laden had where he could hold the various ethnic groups together and keep al-Qaeda unified? Is there anyone who can step up to that? Will it be Zawahiri; will it be someone else? What is the role of someone like Awlaki, who is outside the traditional al-Qaeda structure?

So these are all the questions that I look forward to hearing the answers to. I look forward to the insights of the members of our panel, all of whom have long records of expertise and experience.

I, again, thank all of the witnesses for being here. I thank the Members for having such a large turnout this morning.

With that, I yield to the gentleman from Mississippi, the Ranking Member, Mr. Thompson.

Mr. THOMPSON. Thank you very much, Mr. Chairman, for holding this hearing. I join you in welcoming our panel of witnesses.

Before we consider the risk of a terrorist attack following the death of bin Laden, I want to publicly add my voice to the many who have commended the President, the National security team, and our uniformed forces for successfully completing a mission that began over 10 years ago. The success of this mission was made possible by the administration's efforts with reliable intelligence and the surgical use of force.

For many, the killing of bin Laden has always been the ultimate goal of the war on terror. As the mastermind of the terrorist attacks on September 11, he became the central focus of our policies. Bin Laden became the personification of terrorism for us. We went to war in Afghanistan to eliminate bin Laden's training camps and base of operation. We went to war in Iraq because we were told that Saddam Hussein had some connection with bin Laden. In the last 10 years, many of our policies at home and abroad have been based on forecasts and predictions about bin Laden. For many, the elimination of bin Laden will require a dramatic shift in thinking about and analyzing the terrorist threat.

In the last 10 years, we have seen the migration and mutation of the terrorist network and the terrorist threat. The threat network has moved beyond borders, and operatives have become decentralized. At the time of his death, bin Laden remained a dangerous, charismatic figure, but his control was not absolute, and his authority was not singular. We cannot ignore the new challenges presented by his death. In every group, the death of a leader causes disarray and confusion among the followers. These periods of transition can last for weeks or years.

When we consider the safety of our country, the question that matters most is what will we do while the terrorists are in the throes of transition? For fiscal year 2012, the answer is not encouraging. The DHS appropriations bill recently approved by the Republican-controlled Appropriations Committee cut the Department's budget by more than $1 billion. Since bin Laden's death, we have learned that al-Qaeda was targeting our cities and critical infrastructure. I am glad to see that our Chairman acknowledged the cutting back of some of those desperately needed funds, and I look forward to at some point, Mr. Chairman, working with you on getting many of those funds restored based on this treasure trove of information that was collected at the site of the killing of bin Laden.

Last week the Pakistani Taliban and al-Qaeda-allied groups struck an American armored vehicle transporting American Government personnel. They claimed the attack was in retaliation for bin Laden's death. At a time when our adversaries are seeking opportunities to attack us, cuts in homeland security funding puts us in harm's way. Bin Laden's death does not end the threat to this Nation. In many ways, the picture has become more complex. Our focus must remain steady. Our funding must match our focus.

I look forward to this hearing and to hearing from our witnesses today about the dynamic threat environment we now face.

Mr. Chairman, I yield back.

[The information follows:]

PREPARED STATEMENT OF RANKING MEMBER BENNIE G. THOMPSON

MAY 25, 2011

Before we consider the risk of terrorist attack following the death of bin Laden, I want to publicly add my voice to the many who have commended the President, the National security team and our uniformed forces for successfully completing a mission that began 10 years ago.

The success of this mission was made possible by this administration's efforts, reliable intelligence and the surgical use of force.

For many, the killing of bin Laden has always been the ultimate goal of the war on terror.

As the mastermind of the terrorist attacks on September 11, he became the central focus of our policies.

Bin Laden became the personification of terrorism for us.

We went to war in Afghanistan to eliminate bin Laden's training camps and base of operations.

We went to war in Iraq because we were told that Saddam Hussein had some connection with bin Laden.

In the last 10 years, many of our policies at home and abroad have been based on forecasts and predictions about bin Laden.

For many, the elimination of bin Laden will require a dramatic shift in thinking about and analyzing the terrorist threat.

In the last 10 years, we have seen the migration and mutation of the terrorist network and the terrorist threat.

The terrorist network has moved beyond familiar borders and operatives have become decentralized.

At the time of his death, Bin Laden remained a dangerous charismatic figure, but his control was not absolute and his authority was not singular.

We cannot ignore the new challenge presented by his death.

In every group, the death of a leader causes disarray and confusion among the followers. These periods of transition can last for weeks or years.

When we consider the safety of our country, the question that matters most is—what will we do while the terrorist are in the throes of transition?

For fiscal year 2012, the answer is not encouraging.

The DHS appropriations bill, recently approved by the Republican-controlled Appropriations Committee, cuts the Department's budget by more than $1 billion.

Since bin Laden's death, we have learned that al-Qaeda was targeting our cities and critical infrastructure.

We also know that AQAP is actively targeting our aviation sector.

Last week, the Pakistani Taliban, an al-Qaeda-allied group struck an American armored vehicle transporting American Government personnel. They claimed the attack was in retaliation for bin Laden's death.

At a time when our adversaries are seeking opportunities to attack us, cuts to homeland security funding put us in harm's way.

Bin Laden's death does not end the threat to this Nation.

In many ways, the picture has become more complex. Our focus must remain steady. And our funding must match our focus.

Chairman KING. Thank you, Congressman Thompson.
[The statement of Hon. Richardson follows:]

PREPARED STATEMENT OF HON. LAURA RICHARDSON

MAY 24, 2011

I would like to thank Chairman King and Ranking Member Thompson for convening this hearing today focused on the current state of terror threats to the American Homeland in light of the death of Osama bin Laden. While the death of bin Laden has been a significant victory in the war on terror for America as well as the rest of the world, the implications of this victory need to be addressed. Thus, I would like to thank our distinguished panel of witnesses for appearing before the committee today to discuss these very important issues that lay before us.

The death of bin Laden marks the most significant turning point to date in our Nation's efforts to combat and eliminate al-Qaeda and its worldwide affiliates. As the figurehead and symbol of global terrorism, he inspired thousands of militants and extremists to wage war against the West and commit unspeakable acts of violence.

While it is clear that his death has marked a significant blow to al-Qaeda and its affiliates, most experts agree that bin Laden's death alone is not likely to end the war on terror. In fact, as some of the recent events in Pakistan have indicated, many terrorist groups are not deterred by the recent death of bin Laden and are likely to continue to plot attacks from safe havens world-wide.

As al-Qaeda attempts to regroup and reorganize after the death of bin Laden, their leader, it is important that the United States assess the new threat dynamic in order to ensure our National security efforts remain strong and do not become complacent in the wake of bin Laden's death. This means continuing to focus on al-Qaeda and its affiliates, supporting the message of democracy that is now spreading across the Middle East, and providing our counterterrorism officials with the tools they need in order to build an effective capacity to combat these world-wide threats.

Unfortunately, the fiscal year 2012 Department of Homeland Security (DHS) appropriations bill that was recently approved by the House Homeland Security Appropriations Subcommittee, will make these efforts considerably more difficult with a decrease in funding of $1.1 billion—or 2.6%—below last year's level and $3 billion—or 7%—below the President's request. These proposed cuts represent an unacceptable blow to our National security and could undoubtedly jeopardize future counterterrorism efforts.

As the representative of the 37th district of California, I understand the importance of giving law enforcement officials the resources they need to efficiently and effectively protect our local communities. My Congressional district abuts the Nation's largest ports, contains oil refineries that produce more than 1 million barrels per day, and is home to a number of gas treatment and petrochemical facilities that present a target-rich environment for those seeking to do us harm.

Thus, it is imperative that we continue to provide counterterrorism officials with the resources necessary to sustain their efforts to disrupt, dismantle, and defeat al-Qaeda and strengthen the resilience of our Nation against acts of terrorism.

Thank you again Mr. Chairman and Ranking Member Thompson for convening this very important hearing today. I look forward to hearing from our distinguished panel of witnesses on these issues. I yield back my time.

Chairman KING. Our first witness this morning is former Congressman Lee Hamilton. I had the privilege of serving on the House Foreign Affairs Committee with Congressman Hamilton during his extraordinary career. He was chairman of the House Committee on Foreign Affairs, the House Permanent Select Committee on Intelligence, and everyone in the country knows of his outstanding service as Vice Chair of the 9/11 Commission with Governor Kean. He served on the U.S. Homeland Security Advisory Council and led the Woodrow Wilson International Center for Scholars. He currently serves as co-chair of the Bipartisan Policy Center's National Security Preparedness Group. It has always been a privilege of mine to consider Lee Hamilton a friend and colleague. I certainly welcome you here for your testimony this morning.

Thank you, Chairman Hamilton.

STATEMENT OF LEE HAMILTON, BIPARTISAN POLICY CENTER

Mr. HAMILTON. Thank you, Chairman King and Ranking Member Thompson, and, of course, the other Members of the committee. I am very pleased to have the opportunity to be with you today. I have really appreciated the leadership that the Chairman and the other Members of this committee have shown on the whole question of the terrorist threat confronting the country. I am deeply grateful for the sustained support coming from this committee in reforming our National security institutions.

As the Chairman mentioned, I am appearing today as the co-chair of the Bipartisan Policy Center's National Security Preparedness Group, and very pleased indeed to be joined by two distinguished members of that group, Fran Townsend and Peter Bergen, here at the witness table.

Significant progress has been made, of course, since 9/11 in protecting the homeland, and our country is undoubtedly more safer and more secure. But it also remains the fact that a number of our key recommendations of the Commission have not yet been implemented.

The attacks on 9/11 demonstrated the teamwork and collaboration and effective communications at the site are critical. We have made some movement towards establishing the unity of command. One person has to be in charge when you have a disaster strike. They have to make thousands of decisions very quickly. I have heard simply from too many community leaders and first responders across the Nation that many communities, many regions still have not solved the problem of a unified command structure in the event of a disaster.

Likewise, there has been some, but not sufficient progress in establishing interoperable communications for first responders. I know the Chairman and others on this committee have been very, very good in calling the attention of the country to that. This is a no-brainer. The people at the site of a disaster—the chief players, the police, the first aid people, the experts—all have to be able to communicate with one another, and the Government has to allocate an additional 10 megahertz of the radio spectrum to public safety to enhance the ability to communicate in a disaster.

There have been improvements in transportation and security and border security, but transportation security technology still lags in its capability to screen passengers and baggage for concealed weapons and explosives. Several attempted attacks over the past few years perpetrated by terrorists who could have been detected by the U.S. immigration system demonstrate that a more streamlined terrorist watch-listing capability and improved information sharing among the intelligence agencies and immigration authorities still have to be improved.

One area of significant progress is the deployment of the biometric entry system, known as US–VISIT. But a biometric exit component to determine which foreign nationals have left the United States has not yet been deployed. I think if law enforcement and intelligence officials had known for certain in August 2001, prior to the attack, that two of the 9/11 hijackers remained in the United States, the search for them could have taken on a greater urgency.

With respect to intelligence reform, the Director of National Intelligence has certainly made progress in several areas, including increased information sharing and improved cooperation among the various agencies. But it is not clear that the DNI is the driving force of the intelligence community that the 9/11 Commission envisioned. Some ambiguity still appears in the basic statutory structure over the DNI's authority with regard to budget and personnel. Strengthening his position in these areas would advance the unity of effort in intelligence, whether that be done through legislation or declarations from the President.

A major disappointment for all of us on the 9/11 Commission has been the failure of the administration to empanel the Privacy and Civil Liberties Oversight Board. This was a major recommendation of the Commission, easily agreed to unanimously by all members of the Commission. My information at this time is that the President has only nominated two members to serve on the five-member Board, and neither has been confirmed by the Senate. I thank Ranking Member Thompson and other Members of the committee for the letter that was sent to the administration about the Board's vacancies. I encourage the committee to push that in the months ahead.

Another disappointment, of course, is the failure of this Congress to reform oversight of the intelligence community and the Department of Homeland Security. This committee is well aware, better than almost anybody else, of the fractured oversight of DHS. I need not give the statistics to you. It is an inefficient allocation of limited resources needed to secure our Nation. The massive Department of the DHS will be much better integrated if there is integrated oversight. I know Members of this committee have been helpful on this. I have some understanding of the difficulties of the problem and working it out, but it is really a high priority and a National security interest that the oversight of Homeland Security be much more focused.

The capture and death of Osama bin Laden is the most significant achievement to date in our efforts to defeat al-Qaeda. That hard work, the cooperation, vigilance, the tenacity over a period of years, as both of you in your opening statements have acknowledged, has been critical. There is no question that his capture and death came about as a result of reforms that have recently been enacted in the Federal Government that yielded much closer collaboration and information sharing.

Of course, we now have a major new source of information that the intelligence community can analyze in great detail. I think it is likely that the information that we get is even more important than the death of Osama bin Laden himself.

Whether his death is a turning point in our fight against terrorism remains to be seen. You can kill a man. You cannot kill a symbol. Osama bin Laden is dead. Al-Qaeda is not. It is a network, not a hierarchy, as others have said. Over a period of years, it has been adaptive, it has been resilient, and his death is certainly a setback for al-Qaeda, but likely not its demise. Its affiliates and al-Qaeda itself will almost certainly attempt to avenge his death; however, that attack will not necessarily occur soon.

Al-Qaeda's capabilities, as the Chairman noted, and its ability to implement large-scale attacks are less formidable that they were 10 years ago, but there isn't any doubt at all about al-Qaeda's intent. They want to kill more Americans.

Al-Qaeda has been marked by rapid decentralization. The most significant threats to American security come from affiliates of core al-Qaeda, al-Qaeda in the Arabian Peninsula, al-Qaeda elsewhere. Its influence, which is on the rise in South Asia, continues to extend to failing states like Yemen and Somalia.

In assessing threats to the homeland security, senior U.S. counterterrorism officials now call attention to al-Qaeda's strategy of diversification. Mounting attacks involving a wide variety of perpetrators of different national and ethnic background make it very difficult to profile threats. Most troubling is the pattern of increasing terrorist recruitment of American citizens and residents to act as lone wolves. There were two such attacks in just last year or 2, and it is very distressing that Americans seem to be playing an increasingly prominent role in al-Qaeda's movements.

We know that individuals in the United States are engaging in self-radicalization, which is an alarming development. This process

8

is often influenced by blogs and other on-line content advocating violent extremism. While there are methods to monitor some of this activity, it is simply impossible to know the inner thinking of every at-risk person. Thus, self-radicalization poses, I believe, a grave threat to the United States.

The National Security Preparedness Group will soon release a report with recommendations for improving our defenses to radicalization. That report has not yet been submitted to the full group, but it will be done soon, and I hope it will be helpful to you as you look at this problem.

Because al-Qaeda and its affiliates will not give up, we cannot let our guard down. We will see new attempts and likely successful attacks. We must constantly assess our vulnerabilities and anticipate new lines of attack; not become complacent, but remain vigilant and resolute. We have done a lot. We have done much. We have had a great deal of progress. But there is an awful lot more to do.

Thank you for inviting me to testify to this committee. Most importantly, thank you for the long-standing leadership of this committee on homeland security matters.

Thank you.

[The statement of Mr. Hamilton follows:]

PREPARED STATEMENT OF HON. LEE HAMILTON

MAY 25, 2011

I. INTRODUCTION

Mr. Chairman, Ranking Member Thompson, Members of the committee: I am pleased to have the opportunity to appear before you today. This committee has been at the center of defending the country from the terrorist threat we face. I am deeply grateful to you for your sustained support of the 9/11 Commission's recommendations and leadership in reforming our National security institutions. You have done a great deal to ensure we are taking the difficult steps necessary to confront this determined enemy and protect Americans, our allies, and people throughout the world.

Today, I am appearing in my capacity as a co-chair of the Bipartisan Policy Center's National Security Preparedness Group (NSPG), a successor to the 9/11 Commission. Drawing on a strong roster of National security professionals, the NSPG works as an independent, bipartisan group to monitor the implementation of the 9/11 Commission's recommendations and address other emerging National security issues.

I join in testifying today with two National security experts who also happen to be members of the NSPG, Fran Townsend and Peter Bergen. In addition to them, the NSPG is composed of:

- Governor Tom Kean: Former Governor of New Jersey; Chairman of the 9/11 Commission; and Co-Chair of the National Security Preparedness Group;
- The Honorable E. Spencer Abraham: Former U.S. Secretary of Energy and U.S. Senator from Michigan, The Abraham Group;
- Dr. Stephen Flynn: President, Center for National Policy;
- Dr. John Gannon: BAE Systems, former CIA Deputy Director for Intelligence, Chairman of the National Intelligence Council, and U.S. House Homeland Security Staff Director;
- The Honorable Dan Glickman: Former Secretary of Agriculture and U.S. Congressman;
- Dr. Bruce Hoffman: Georgetown University terrorism specialist;
- The Honorable Dave McCurdy: Former Congressman from Oklahoma and Chairman of the U.S. House Intelligence Committee, President of the American Gas Association;
- The Honorable Edwin Meese III: Former U.S. Attorney General, Ronald Reagan Distinguished Fellow in Public Policy and Chairman of the Center for Legal and Judicial Studies at The Heritage Foundation;

- The Honorable Tom Ridge: Former Governor of Pennsylvania and U.S. Secretary of Homeland Security, Senior Advisor at Deloitte Global LLP, Ridge Global;
- The Honorable Richard L. Thornburgh: Former U.S. Attorney General, Of Counsel at K&L Gates; and
- The Honorable Jim Turner: Former Congressman from Texas and Ranking Member of the U.S. House Homeland Security Committee, Arnold and Porter, LLP.

In recent months, our group has sponsored the following events:
- BPC Domestic Intelligence Conference featuring FBI Director Mueller and DNI Director Clapper—October 2010.
- Bridge-Builder Breakfast: Addressing America's Intelligence Challenges in a Bipartisan Way with House Intelligence Committee Chairman Rogers and Ranking Member Ruppersberger—March 2011.
- Press conference marking the release of the Bipartisan Policy Center's National Security Preparedness Group report, Assessing the Terrorist Threat—September 2010.

We will soon release another report with recommendations for improving initiatives to prevent violent radicalization in the United States.

We believe the depth of this group's experience on National security issues can be of assistance to you and the Executive branch and we look forward to continuing to work with you.

II. SIGNIFICANT PROGRESS HAS BEEN MADE IN ADDRESSING THREATS TO THE AMERICAN HOMELAND SINCE 9/11, YET IMPORTANT 9/11 COMMISSION RECOMMENDATIONS REMAIN UNFULFILLED

Effect of the 9/11 Attacks

The terrorist attacks of September 11, 2001 had a profoundly dramatic impact on Government, the private sector, and our daily lives. The suddenness of the attacks on American soil and the loss of so many lives, made us feel vulnerable in our homes and caused us to question whether our Government was properly organized to protect us from this lethal threat. The economic damage resulting from the attacks was severe. In short order, we shifted from a "peace dividend" at the end of the Cold War to the expenditure of massive amounts of taxpayer dollars on new security measures.

The consequences of the attacks for the private sector have been striking. More than 80% of our Nation's critical infrastructure is owned by the private sector, and protecting it from terrorist operations has become an urgent priority. Working together, the Government and private sector have improved their information sharing and thus our security posture.

Businesses in all sectors have adapted to this new reality. They have focused on how best to protect personnel and our food and water supplies; prepared continuity plans in preparation for possible disruptions; and altered how buildings are constructed, adopting innovative safety features. U.S. importers, working with the Department of Homeland Security, have pioneered new ways to ensure the integrity of shipping containers that bring goods into the country. The insurance industry's risk analysis has evolved to reflect new realities. These necessary innovations have increased the costs of doing business. Future innovations responding to the evolving threat may raise costs higher.

The Government's Response

Over the past 10 years, our Government's response to the challenge of transnational terrorism has been equally dramatic. Legal, policy, and cultural barriers between agencies created serious impediments to information sharing before the 9/11 attacks. The 9/11 Commission made a number of specific recommendations to improve information sharing across our Government, and many of these have been accepted and implemented, in whole or in part.

Information sharing within the Federal Government, and among Federal, State, local, and Tribal authorities, and with allies, while not perfect, has been considerably improved since 9/11. The level of cooperation among all levels of Government is higher than ever. The CIA, FBI, and the broader intelligence community have implemented significant reforms. In 2004, Congress created the Office of the Director of National Intelligence and the National Counterterrorism Center to ensure unity of effort in the intelligence community. This was a major step toward improved information sharing.

State and local officials have a far greater understanding not only of the threat and how to respond to it, but also, their communities and those who may be at risk of radicalization. There are now 105 Joint Terrorism Task Forces throughout the Nation, and 72 Fusion Centers in which Federal, State, local, and Tribal authorities investigate terrorism leads and share information. Since 2004, DHS has provided more than $340 million in funding to the Fusion Centers. Information sharing with the private sector has also become routine and is an important part of our defenses.

An enormous amount of intelligence information constantly pours into our National security system. And as evidence that there is still room for improvement in handling this information, we saw missed opportunities to stop the Christmas day bomber from boarding Northwest Flight 253, as well as opportunities to intervene before the Fort Hood shootings. But as a result of reforms in the last decade, many plots have been disrupted and many terrorist operatives, including Osama bin Laden, have been brought to justice.

Unfulfilled 9/11 Commission Recommendations

Despite the progress in information sharing and in other areas, important 9/11 Commission recommendations remain unfulfilled. The 9/11 attacks demonstrated that teamwork, collaboration, and effective communications at the site of a disaster are critical. Movement has been made toward establishing a unity of command with one person in charge of directing the efforts of multiple agencies. I have heard, however, from too many community leaders and first responders that many regions still have not solved the problem of having a unified command structure.

There also has been inadequate progress in establishing interoperable communications for first responders. That is why it is vital that the Government allocate an additional 10 megahertz of radio spectrum to public safety that will enhance their ability to communicate during a disaster. I want to recognize the leadership that Chairman King and Ranking Member Thompson and many Members of this committee have shown in supporting a bill that will achieve this goal.

There have been improvements in transportation security and border security. However, transportation security technology still lags in its capability to screen passengers and baggage for concealed weapons and explosives. And several attempted attacks over the past 2 years perpetrated by terrorists who could have been detected by the U.S. immigration system demonstrate that a more streamlined terrorist watchlisting capability and improved information sharing between intelligence agencies and immigration authorities must be implemented.

One area of significant progress is the deployment of the biometric entry system known as US–VISIT. But a biometric exit component of US–VISIT to determine which foreign nationals have left the United States has not yet been deployed. If law enforcement and intelligence officials had known for certain in August and September 2001 that two of the 9/11 hijackers remained in the United States, the search for them might have taken on greater urgency.

With respect to intelligence reform, the Director of National Intelligence has made progress in several areas: Increased information sharing, better analysis of intelligence, improved cooperation among agencies, and sharpened collection priorities. But it still is not clear that the DNI is the driving force for intelligence community integration that the Commission envisioned. Some ambiguity appears to remain with respect to the DNI's authority over budget and personnel. Strengthening the DNI's position in these areas would advance the unity of effort in intelligence, whether through legislation or with repeated declarations from the President that the DNI is the unequivocal leader of the intelligence community.

I also want to recognize that the FBI has gone through dramatic change and has had strong leadership under Director Mueller. It continues to move in a positive direction from a focus strictly on law enforcement to preventing terrorism. This is a significant cultural change that can be furthered by placing the status of intelligence analysts on par with special agents, who have traditionally risen to management at the Bureau.

The CIA has improved its intelligence analysis and removed barriers between its analysts and operations officers. But recruiting well-placed sources remains difficult and the CIA has had difficulty recruiting officers qualified with the language skills where there is the greatest need. Congress can help in the language area by supporting programs that teach young people proficiency in foreign languages.

A major disappointment has been the failure of the administration to empanel the Privacy and Civil Liberties Oversight Board. This was a major 9/11 Commission recommendation that was strongly supported by all Commissioners. At this time, the President has only nominated two members to serve on the five-member Board, and neither of them has been confirmed by the Senate. I commend Ranking Member Thompson and other Members of the committee for the letter that they sent to the administration about the Board's vacancies and encourage this committee to continue to push the administration on this issue.

Another disappointment is the failure of Congress to reform oversight of the intelligence community and the Department of Homeland Security. The Commission recommended that Congress create a Joint Committee for Intelligence or create House and Senate Committees with the combined authorizing and appropriation powers. While these changes have not been implemented, a positive step was the House Intelligence Committee Chairman's commitment to include three Members of the House Appropriations Committee in Intelligence Committee hearings and briefings.

As this committee is well aware, oversight of the Department of Homeland Security remains fractured. In 2009 alone, DHS officials answered 11,680 letters, provided 2,058 briefings, and sent 232 witnesses to 166 hearings. This amounted to about 66 work years responding to questions from Congress, at a cost to taxpayers of about $10 million. This is an inefficient allocation of limited resources needed to secure our Nation. Moreover, the massive Department will be better integrated if there is integrated oversight.

III. THE CAPTURE OF OSAMA BIN LADEN AND THE THREAT PICTURE AFTER HIS DEATH

The Bin Laden Operation

The capture of Osama bin Laden is a significant achievement of the United States intelligence and military forces—the most significant achievement to date in our efforts to defeat al-Qaeda. The raid took hard work, cooperation, vigilance, and tenacity, over a period of years. It involved surveillance, analysis of many bits of information, interceptions, and the extraordinary skills of our Special Operations Forces. The CIA and the military worked together seamlessly. The raid was a culmination of intense and tireless efforts on the part of many dedicated National security personnel over a period of many years.

It was a highly complex, innovative, and clandestine operation that led us to Osama bin Laden. We would get a bit of intelligence from one source, carefully analyze it, and then use it to drive further efforts and operations. A simple intercepted phone call proved critically important when the response to the caller said, "I'm back with the people I was with before"—that is, he had returned to Osama bin Laden.

It used the full range of our capabilities, both in collecting intelligence from human and technical sources, and subjecting it to very rigorous analysis by our Government's leading experts on bin Laden and his organization. There is no question that his capture came about as a result of reforms that have recently been enacted in the Federal Government that yielded much closer collaboration and sharing of information among intelligence components and the military. That cooperation paid dividends that assisted in locating bin Laden's hiding place.

And we now have a major source of new information that the intelligence community will analyze in very great detail. The trove of information—the captured hard drive and documents—recovered from his compound may eventually be even more important than his death.

Bin Laden's Death

Osama bin Laden was the most infamous terrorist of our time. He was also the most successful. He brought together terrorist elements under one movement, al-Qaeda. Most remarkably, as the mastermind of 9/11, he persuaded 19 young men to go to their deaths for a cause. He also directed the attacks on the American embassies in East Africa.

There is some difference of opinion on his role at his death. My personal view is that for the last decade, Osama bin Laden has been a figurehead more than a mastermind. I do not think that a man without a telephone or access to the internet, relying on couriers, could have been a prime mover in more recent terrorist operations. There can be no doubt about his symbolic importance.

The single act of his death does not change everything—nothing ever changes everything—it does not, for example, resolve two messy wars. We should receive some satisfaction from his death, but not exaltation. Men die, symbols do not. In his death, he can still inspire terrorist attacks. But it is worth noting that in the Middle East, news of his death was greeted with ambivalence, and even indifference.

Future of al-Qaeda

Whether it is a turning point in our fight against terrorism remains to be seen. Although Osama bin Laden is dead, al-Qaeda is not—it is a network, not a hierarchy. Over a period of years, al-Qaeda has been very adaptive and resilient. Bin Laden's death is certainly a setback for al-Qaeda but likely not its demise.

Al-Qaeda will be searching for an effective leader. Its likely next leader, Ayman al-Zawahiri, will almost certainly struggle to keep al-Qaeda relevant. He is likely to be the last man standing in the struggle for leadership. We should not underestimate Zawahiri. He is extremely pious, ruthless; he is not a lightweight; he has been instrumental in al-Qaeda's strategy, development, and evolution over a period of years.

Al-Qaeda's capabilities to implement large-scale attacks are less formidable than they were 10 years ago, but al-Qaeda continues to have the intent and reach to kill dozens, or even hundreds, of Americans in a single attack. The war against terror is not won. The work is not done. It is not time to declare victory.

Al-Qaeda and its affiliates will almost certainly attempt to avenge him. They will not necessarily attack soon. The threat from al-Qaeda is more diverse and more complex than ever—although less severe than the catastrophic proportions of the 9/11 attacks. It continues to hope to inflict mass casualties in the United States

Al-Qaeda has been marked by rapid decentralization. The most significant threats to American National security come from the affiliates of core al-Qaeda—like al-Qaeda in the Arabian Peninsula under U.S.-born Anwar al-Awlaki's leadership. Al-Qaeda's influence is also on the rise in South Asia and continues to extend into failing or failed states such as Yemen and Somalia.

In assessing terrorist threats to the American homeland, senior U.S. counterterrorism officials now call attention to al-Qaeda's strategy of "diversification"—mounting attacks involving a wide variety of perpetrators of different National and ethnic backgrounds that cannot easily be "profiled" as threats. Lone wolves, who are not connected to formal terrorist organizations, are the most difficult to detect, in part because they do not fit any particular ethnic, economic, educational, or social profile.

Most troubling, we have seen a pattern of increasing terrorist recruitment of American citizens and residents. In 2009, there were two actual terrorist attacks on our soil. The Fort Hood shooting, claimed the lives of 13 people, and a U.S. military recruiter was killed in Little Rock, Arkansas. Indeed, many counterterrorism experts consider 2010 the "year of the homegrown terrorist." Last year, 10 Muslim-Americans plotted against domestic targets, and 5 actually carried out their plots. Today, we know that Americans are playing increasingly prominent roles in al-Qaeda's movement. And Muslim-American youth are being recruited in Somali communities in Minneapolis and Portland, Oregon, in some respects moving the front lines to the interior of our country.

Moreover, we know that individuals in the U.S. are engaging in "self-radicalization," which is an alarming development. This process is often influenced by blogs and other on-line content advocating violent Islamist extremism. While there are methods to monitor some of this activity, it is simply impossible to know the inner thinking of every at-risk person. Thus, self-radicalization poses a grave threat in the United States, and as I noted earlier, our National Security Preparedness Group will soon release a report with recommendations for improving our defenses to radicalization.

Because al-Qaeda and its affiliates will not give up, we cannot let our guard down. We must not become complacent, but remain vigilant and resolute.

Evolving Mechanisms for Attacking the United States

Our enemy continues to probe our vulnerabilities and design innovative ways to attack us. Such innovation is best exemplified by the discovery in October 2010 of explosives packed in toner cartridges, addressed to synagogues in Chicago, and shipped on Fed Ex and UPS cargo flights from Yemen. This plot constituted an assault on our international transportation and commerce delivery systems. And it was done without the terrorists ever having to set foot within the United States. Although it failed, terrorists will not abandon efforts to develop new ways to inflict great harm on us.

Another way that terrorists can attack without ever physically crossing our borders is through a cyber attack. Successive DNIs have warned that the cyber threat to critical infrastructure systems—to electrical, financial, water, energy, food supply, military, and telecommunications networks—is grave. Earlier this month, senior DHS officials described a "nightmare scenario" of a terrorist group hacking into United States computer systems and disrupting our electric grid, shutting down power to large swathes of the country, perhaps for as long as several weeks. As the current crisis in Japan demonstrates, disruption of power grids and basic infrastructure can have devastating effects on society.

This is not science fiction. It is possible to take down cyber systems and trigger cascading side effects. Defending the United States against such attacks must be an urgent priority.

IV. INTERNATIONAL IMPLICATIONS

The capture and removal of Osama bin Laden raises many urgent questions. Among them are the following:

What is the future of the U.S.-Pakistan relationship? The discovery of bin Laden in a large compound adjacent to a Pakistani Army cantonment, just a 2-hour drive from the Pakistani capital, and about a mile from Pakistan's West Point—not in a remote area over which the government has limited control—requires answers from the Pakistani government about whether its intelligence service, military, or other officials were aware of bin Laden's whereabouts for some time, possibly even providing support. It is difficult to imagine that bin Laden would have chosen to live in Abbottabad unless he had some assurance of protection from Pakistan military and intelligence officials. There is intense debate over how hard to press Pakistan for answers about bin Laden and what Pakistani officials knew.

While Pakistan has cooperated with U.S. counterterrorism efforts, relations with Pakistan have been strained in recent years. The United States has provided large amounts of aid to Pakistan in return for its assistance in hunting down al-Qaeda leaders, but Pakistan has been known to look both ways—helping the United States and the Taliban as well.

Pakistan has been less than a full partner in our counterterrorism efforts and in Afghanistan. Pakistan's government has long been internally divided about terrorism. Parts of its government are sympathetic to terrorism, parts are unwilling to act aggressively against it, and other parts are either incompetent or playing a double game with and against terrorism. U.S. officials are now openly skeptical about Pakistan's commitment to countering terrorist activity within their borders, and they question whether Pakistan will be a better partner in identifying and apprehending terrorists in the future.

For its part, Pakistan will likely continue to demand that the United States stop encroachments upon its sovereignty in counterterrorism operations. Thus, the death of Osama bin Laden may very well, in the short run, strengthen the extremists.

This difficult and complex relationship with Pakistan must be managed, not dissolved, in order to advance our shared interests in countering terrorism and ending the war in Afghanistan. The U.S.-Pakistan relationship is central to the interests of both countries. The United States needs cooperation with Pakistan in its fight against terrorism in Afghanistan and ending the war there. Pakistan provides a vital transit link for goods destined for U.S. forces in Afghanistan, and its collapse, with internal terrorist groups and nuclear weapons, could be catastrophic. This is already one of the most difficult bilateral relationships in the world, which has been made worse by recent events. We can only manage it, we cannot resolve all the tensions.

After many demands to cut aid to Pakistan, extensive efforts are now underway to ease tensions between the two countries. In the end, the United States will need to be committed to working with Pakistan despite the lingering questions. Of this we can be sure: More tense times lie ahead in the U.S.-Pakistan relationship. Our focus must be on long-term interests, not short-term frustration. We need a healthy Pakistan that fights extremism and terror, and that means we should help democratic forces within Pakistan.

Another question is Afghanistan. Osama bin Laden's death creates new opportunities to begin real negotiations to end the conflict. The situation there is not good. The United States can clear and hold any area—but only for as long as we stay there. The Taliban have been pushed back, but they are not close to being defeated. Our gains are fragile and reversible. And the corruption and incompetence of the Karzai government is well-known.

With bin Laden's death, U.S. policymakers may be in a position to consider whether a political deal can be cut with the Taliban, which, from our view would require: (1) The Taliban to turn over al-Qaeda leaders, (2) maintaining progress that has been made in Afghanistan towards a more open society, and (3) bringing an end to the war. We can get to that deal by more fighting. Or we can get to a deal by negotiating a political settlement. Success in Afghanistan is not easy to define, but it includes establishing an Afghan government that, in time, can hold off the Taliban with a modest amount of American support and help.

A third issue is whether and how recent events in the Middle East—the so-called Arab Spring—may counter the violent extremist agenda of al-Qaeda and its affiliates. Al-Qaeda has been unsuccessful in its attempts to destabilize Arab governments and replace them with a Muslim Caliphate that stretches across the region. It has not been relevant to the revolutionary waves sweeping the Middle East. Where al-Qaeda failed, peaceful protesters have succeeded through their grassroots uprisings in achieving regime change and dramatic political reforms. What is erupting today in the Middle East is profoundly important—a quest for freedom, for personal dignity, for justice, for a better life. These demands are not going to fade away.

But these revolutions are not without risks. It is by no means clear that they will succeed. If they falter and fail to destroy repressive governments and to build a new democratic world, al-Qaeda and other violent extremist groups could emerge again.

In any event, we are headed for a more uncertain Arab world.

Today Muslim people have a chance, with real elections, constitutions, and political parties. If the people want and demand democratic change and accountable governments, no government will be able to resist. None of us can predict the outcome, but we of course can hope for, and support, more democratic regimes.

The United States must seize the opportunity provided by the Arab Spring, welcome the changes toward self-determination and opportunity, oppose violence and repression, promote reform toward democracy, and support economic development for the nations moving in a democratic direction.

Public diplomacy (and nontraditional diplomacy more broadly) may also be a useful tool in facilitating the change sweeping through the region. We should seek to foster reform, forestall gross human rights violations, and work closely with the international community, while avoiding putting the American imprimatur on the protests.

The key will be to engage pragmatically with the governments of the region to help them build stable institutions and provide immediate economic improvement to their people. We should support an agenda of opportunity for the Islamic world. People-to-people exchanges—between legislators, businesspeople, students, academics, civil servants, trade unions, lawyers, scientists, and other groups—could be very productive here. In the 9/11 Commission Report, we recommended that the United States "rebuild the scholarship, exchange, and library programs that reach out to young people and offer them knowledge and hope." A significant exchange program for emerging Middle East and North Africa democracies should be a relatively easy lift for Congress, and would be a tangible way of signaling U.S. friendship to the new democracies, on the basis of mutual respect and without seeming to meddle or to seek control.

The United States and European Union should also work together to use trade and aid policies to give a quick economic assist, in terms of market access, to the new democratic governments (once they emerge). Such an initiative would be much more effective if done in concert with the European Union.

V. CONCLUSION

Significant progress has been made since 9/11, and our country is undoubtedly safer and more secure. We have damaged our enemy, but the ideology of violent Islamist extremism is alive and attracting new adherents, including right here in our own country. Close cooperation with American Muslim communities is the key to preventing the domestic radicalization that has troubled some of our European allies. Positive outreach and efforts to foster mutual understanding are the best way to prevent radicalization and sustain collaborative relationships.

Our terrorist adversaries and the tactics and techniques they employ are evolving rapidly. We will see new attempts, and likely successful attacks. One of our major deficiencies before the 9/11 attacks was that our National security agencies were not changing at the accelerated rate required by a new and different kind of enemy. We must not make that mistake again.

The terrorist threat will be with us far into the future, demanding that we be ever vigilant. Our National security departments require strong leadership and attentive management at every level to ensure that all parts are working well together, that there is innovation and imagination. Our agencies and their dedicated workforces have gone through much change and we commend them for their achievements in protecting the American people. But there is a tendency toward inertia in all bureaucracies. Vigorous Congressional oversight is imperative to ensure that they remain vigilant and continue to pursue needed reforms.

Our task is difficult. We must constantly assess our vulnerabilities and anticipate new lines of attack. We have done much, but there is much more to do.

Thank you for inviting me to testify, and for this committee's long-standing leadership on these critical issues.

Chairman KING. Thank you, Chairman Hamilton.

Our next witness is a long-time friend, fellow New Yorker, whose mother is a constituent of mine. So I figured I would be very polite to you today, which I would be anyway, especially with your mother watching.

Very seriously, Fran Townsend is a career Federal prosecutor with a very distinguished record in the field of counterterrorism in several administrations, not just in the Justice Department, but in the Coast Guard and in the White House as President George Bush's principal counterterrorism advisor. She is currently senior vice president at MacAndrews & Forbes Holdings, is a National security contributor and analyst, and she serves on the President's Intelligence Advisory Board.

Fran, it is great to have you here today, and thank you for all your service. I certainly look forward to your testimony.

STATEMENT OF FRANCES F. TOWNSEND, SENIOR VICE PRESIDENT, WORLDWIDE GOVERNMENT, LEGAL AND BUSINESS AFFAIRS, MACANDREWS & FORBES HOLDINGS, INC.

Ms. TOWNSEND. Thank you, Mr. Chairman, Ranking Member Thompson, and Members of the committee. Thank you very much for inviting me here today.

Before I begin to address the topic at hand, it seems to me that though we are discussing today threats to the United States from terror, the impact of natural disasters like that in Missouri have captured our hearts and prayers. I know that we all, I think, pray for the victims, families, and the missing.

I have to say it is a special privilege for me to be here with you all today. Like many who devoted a substantial part of their professional lives in the hunt for bin Laden and to bring him to justice, it is especially satisfying to be with you to consider now the threats we face in a world rid of him. In discussing the threat we face, we must consider the role bin Laden played. Bin Laden was at the heart of what counterterrorism professionals refer to as the al-Qaeda core. Bin Laden was the father, the founder, and ideological author. He was, as the name of the organization suggests, the base.

Our understanding of bin Laden's role was imperfect and evolved over time. While he was always viewed as a charismatic inspirational figure, key to recruitment, fundraising, ideology, and leadership, the U.S. view of his operational role was unclear. Bin Laden inspired loyalty from affiliates like al-Qaeda in the Islamic Maghreb and al-Qaeda in the Arabian Peninsula, who swore allegiance, or bayat, to him. He had a direct hand in cases like the 1998 East Africa embassy bombings and September 11.

For years after 9/11, it was believed he played a less active role until, of course, last year, when he seemed to have had a more direct role in the summer 2010 threat in Europe. Since the raid on the bin Laden compound in Abbottabad, public reports indicate bin Laden has played a more active operational role, encouraging attacks against the United States and targeting Americans worldwide. There have been warnings about attack plans against railways, reports of a potential attack against oil tankers, and we should expect more such warnings from the Government in the coming days.

But we should understand many of these targets were aspirational. They were being considered. There had been past attacks against rail in London and Madrid, and, of course, the al-Qaeda attack against the MV Limburg, so that such plans were being considered and discussed is not surprising. That bin Laden played an active operational role makes his sudden absence from al-Qaeda more devastating for them. We know now that bin Laden was focused on attacking the United States, so his death is not only justice for the victims of September 11, the USS Cole, and East Africa bombings, America is safer because he is dead.

So the question is, what remains? I break it down basically into two categories: Who is a threat to us; and, second, where does that threat emanate from?

First, the who. There are three main categories, in my mind, of who directly threatens the United States. First, there are the remnants of the al-Qaeda core; second, the al-Qaeda affiliates; and then last, the other extremist groups.

First, what remains of the al-Qaeda core? Ayman al-Zawahiri, bin Laden's deputy; recently we have heard again of Saif al-Adel, who has resurfaced. But al-Qaeda has failed to name a new leader because there is an internal power struggle. There was no agreed-upon succession plan. There is no one of bin Laden's stature to inspire and guide operations and quell disputes. The al-Qaeda core without bin Laden is badly weakened. The chaos at the top of al-Qaeda is an important targeting opportunity for the United States.

The second category of "who" is perhaps more immediately dangerous to the United States. The second "who" are the al-Qaeda affiliates and, most importantly, al-Qaeda in the Arabian Peninsula, headed by the American-born cleric Anwar al-Awlaki. Intelligence and counterterrorism officials have rightly described al-Qaeda in the Arabian Peninsula, or AQAP, as the most immediate threat to the United States homeland. AQAP has both the intent to attack and had demonstrated some capability. AQAP was behind the Nidal Hasan Fort Hood event, the attempted Christmas day underwear bomber, and the recent computer cartridges attempt.

Awlaki is a serious threat. Unlike Zawahiri, he is a charismatic and inspirational leader. He uses the internet and taped lectures to recruit and radicalize world-wide. There are other affiliates that I won't go into in depth, one in North Africa, those in Somalia, and Asia, but AQAP poses the most immediate threat.

The third category of "who" are other extremist groups: The Pakistan Taliban, which was responsible for the training of the Times Square bomber. Mullah Omar and the Quetta Shura remain our enemy and a direct threat. We must be careful not to write off radical groups that appear only regionally or locally focused, as was the initial belief of the Pakistan Taliban. Lashkar-e-Taiba, LET, which was behind the Mumbai attack, is currently the subject of the trial in Chicago right now. The Haqqani network in the Pakistan tribal areas continues to target and kill coalition forces in Afghanistan.

Last among these other groups, we must not forget Hezbollah. Although a Shiite extremist group, they remain bankrolled by Iran, and prior to September 11 were responsible for killing more Americans than any other terror group. They are armed, militarily capable, deployed world-wide, and remain a significant threat.

The next category that I mentioned is the "where" the threat emanates from. Again, I will talk about three concerns: First, ungoverned or weakly governed states or places; threats inside the United States; and, third, complacency.

First, ungoverned or weakly governed states and places. That was Afghanistan of the 1990s, where al-Qaeda planned and trained. Today we see hotspots in Somalia along the Mali-Mauritania border, in Yemen, and in Pakistan. I know from my own experience both Yemen and Pakistan are frustrating and at times duplicitous partners, but events this week require that I raise a note of caution. The sophisticated Pakistan Taliban attack on the Karachi Naval Air Base suggests a weaker and more humiliated Pakistan military than was previously thought. We must remember that Pakistan has a nuclear arsenal, and, as both President Obama and President Bush have said, the greatest threat to our security is a terrorist group like the Pakistan Taliban with a nuclear weapon.

While it is right that we reevaluate our bilateral relationship with Pakistan, especially given the testimony this week in the Chicago case that shows a link between the Pakistani Intelligence Service and the LET terror group, we must carefully consider what are the alternatives and consequences to the partnership with Pakistan.

There is another weakly-governed space I must mention, though it is not a traditional geographic space. You cannot find it on a map. That is cyberspace and the internet. For all the enormous good of the internet, al-Qaeda and other terrorist groups have learned to use it to their advantage to recruit, to train, to radicalize, and to fundraise. Every plot we uncovered during my time in Government, computers were used. Just by way of example, al Awlaki communicated via the internet with the Fort Hood shooter, and bin Laden had the computers in his compound.

The United States has tremendous capability, and a lot of important work has been done in this area across both the Bush and Obama administrations. Our soldiers and counterterrorism professionals know this is a new 21st-Century battlefield just as any other geography where we fight. It is important the Congress and the American people understand we are fighting there to.

The second "where" is here inside the United States. As the United States has strengthened its border screening, al-Qaeda has made it a priority to recruit Americans and permanent residents who more easily cross our borders. This threats manifests itself with single individuals who attempt attacks, again, like Fort Hood, Times Square, and Christmas day attacks, or in small groups like the Najibullah Zazi case against the New York City subway with backpack bombs.

The last, "where" does the threat come from, doesn't fit easily into any of these categories, but it is equally pernicious and dangerous, and that is the threat of complacency. Killing bin Laden was a difficult and courageous decision by President Obama and an enormous success for the Nation, but the global war on terror is by no means over. Regardless of what you call it, the fight continues because our enemies continue. We won an important and decisive battle, but the threat remains. We have seized the momentum, but we must not think this means we can reduce the investments that produced this success. Our intelligence, military, and law enforcement agencies need the budget and legal authorities to succeed.

18

There is an important vote today in the Senate extending the PATRIOT Act, and while I believe it should have been permanently extended, it must be extended for the next 4 years. The IDENT database should be properly funded. We must prevent terrorists from getting nuclear or other biological weapons, and that means we must ensure we have the ability to respond by maintaining the Strategic National Stockpile and our other unique operational capabilities.

In this time of continued financial crisis, there will be pressure to find cuts. My caution to you is that all cuts are not equal. Capability is built over time. What we found in the immediate aftermath of 9/11 is that it cannot be quickly reacquired in a crisis. President Obama's courageous decision to authorize the bin Laden raid was enabled by an intelligence community whose budget and capability was doubled over the last decade, and this mission was executed by warriors better resourced and trained over the last 10 years. You get what you pay for, and to use the phrase from the MasterCard commercial, the killing of bin Laden was priceless. It was the accomplishment of a Nation and a moment of National pride. We unequivocally told the world: No matter how difficult the task nor how long the journey, we will never forget.

Thank you, Mr. Chairman, for the privilege to testify today. I thank the American people for the privilege of serving them for more than 20 years.

Chairman KING. Thank you.

Our next witness is Peter Bergen, who I assume is the only one in this room that has actually was face-to-face with bin Laden. I think you were the first Western broadcast journalist to interview him. You wrote the book "The Osama bin Laden I Know" and also "The Longest War". Obviously, you have a tremendous depth of insight, knowledge, and a career of expertise. I look forward to your testimony today, as always, and thank you for once again being back before the committee.

STATEMENT OF PETER BERGEN, DIRECTOR, NATIONAL SECURITY STUDIES PROGRAM, NEW AMERICA FOUNDATION

Mr. BERGEN. Thank you, Chairman King, thank you, Ranking Member Thompson, thank you to the Members of the committee, for the privilege of testifying here.

The death of Osama bin Laden is hard to undervalue, as Representative Hamilton and Fran Townsend have already made clear. But just to amplify what they said, when you join al-Qaeda, you don't swear an oath of allegiance to al-Qaeda or al Qaedism. You swear a personal oath of allegiance to bin Laden himself.

There are many differences between al-Qaeda and the Nazi Party, but there is one similarity. When you join the Nazi Party, you didn't swear an oath of allegiance to nazism. You swore a personal oath to Adolph Hitler. When Adolph Hitler died, nazism essentially died with him. Now, I am not going to make the claim that al-Qaeda is going to die with the death of bin Laden or al-Qaedism or bin Ladenism or whatever you want to call it, but you cannot underestimate how important this is.

In 1988, bin Laden and about a dozen other guys founded al-Qaeda. It was, of course, bin Laden's idea to attack the United

States on 9/11. He has been the founder of this group throughout its history, he has been the leader of the group through its history, and he is the intellectual author of the 9/11 attacks. It was, after all, against a lot of internal advice and dissent he pushed the idea of attacking the United States.

We now know from documents recovered and from Representative Hamilton's work on the 9/11 Commission that there were plenty of people in al-Qaeda who said actually attacking the United States is going to be pretty counterproductive, and it turned out to be very counterproductive. Yet bin Laden, was able—because he enjoyed what Khalid Sheikh Mohammed, the operational commander of 9/11, called—in testimony he put in the Zacarias Moussaoui trial, he pointed out that when bin Laden decided something and 98 percent of the Shura Council of al-Qaeda was against him, it was bin Laden's way or the highway. So take this guy out of the equation, this is very damaging for al-Qaeda core.

Who can replace him? Representative King suggested we talk a little bit about that. Ayman al-Zawahiri, the No. 2, is, of course, his deputy. But as Fran Townsend pointed out, there is no official succession plan. According to reporting that I did for CNN, there is an interim leader of al-Qaeda—Fran also mentioned him—Saif al-Adel. He is a former colonel in the Egyptian Special Forces. Al-Qaeda recognizes that it is kind of embarrassing that they haven't appointed a succession leader, and so there was an interim person to take over, perhaps to grease the skids for Ayman al-Zawahiri, who is also an Egyptian, to take over the organization. But, in a way, the best thing that could happen for the United States and for the civilized world is for Ayman al-Zawahiri to take over al-Qaeda because he would run what remains of the organization into the ground.

If you remember Abu Musab al-Zarqawi's death in 2006, the people who replaced him heading al-Qaeda in Iraq were nowhere near as potent in al-Qaeda in Iraq, which basically ceased being an effective insurgent organization while retaining some capabilities today.

So the death of bin Laden, we just want to underline how important it is.

A second point which hasn't been mentioned hitherto is in the Arab Spring, because if al-Qaeda was a huge nail in the coffin of al-Qaeda the organization, the Arab Spring is a massive nail in the coffin of al-Qaeda ideology. Al-Qaeda, the ideology, was already losing steam before the Arab Spring; support for bin Laden, al-Qaeda, and suicide bombings being cratering around the Muslim world for the very good reason that Muslims have noticed that most of the victims of al-Qaeda or allies have been Muslims themselves, which is not impressive for groups that position themselves as the defender of Islam. But the Arab Spring underlines this losing the war of ideas in the Muslim world that has been going on for some period of time.

One very striking thing to me is we haven't seen a single picture of bin Laden carried by the protesters in Cairo or Benghazi or any other city in the Middle East. We haven't seen a single American flag burning, which was so pro forma in that part of the world. We haven't seen a single Israeli flag burning. Al-Qaeda's foot soldiers' ideas and their hope for outcomes are just not part of the conversation.

That said—and these are all very, very good pieces of news that we shouldn't look the gift horse in the face, in a sense—threats do remain. I think that Fran has already mentioned al-Qaeda in the Arabian Peninsula. I am not going to go over that same territory. But I think the death of bin Laden doesn't really affect the operations of al-Qaeda in the Arabian Peninsula. I don't think it really affects the operations of al Shabab. I don't think it really affects the operations of al-Qaeda in Iraq. I don't think it really affects the operations al-Qaeda in the Islamic Maghreb. These groups don't have—most of them, absent al-Qaeda in the Arabian Peninsula—don't have huge capabilities. Al Shabab has been able to attack in Uganda and also in Denmark, so it has shown some ability of outer barrier operations. Al-Qaeda in Iraq had some role, it looks like, in the Glasgow airport attack and also the attacks on the American-owned hotels in Jordan in 2005. But the point is these groups have been constrained in their ability to attack the American homeland.

My final point, because I have run out of time, the New America Foundation and Maxwell School at Syracuse University have looked at the 180 jihadist terrorist attacks in the United States since 9/11, and there is some really strikingly good news and some bad news in this analysis. Only 17 Americans have been killed by a jihadist terrorist since 9/11, which is a pretty striking number, given the kind of fears we had after 9/11. Not one of the cases we looked at involved chemical, biological, radiological, or nuclear weapons, also kind of a strikingly good finding, given the fears we had of that after 9/11. That said, we have had some pretty serious near misses. The Chairman mentioned Najibullah Zazi. We had Faisal Shahzad. We had Abdulmutallab. So these groups retained some capabilities.

One final point on all this. The cases we looked at really spiked in 2009 and 2010. We found 76 cases out of the 180. Just to end on a sort of optimistic note, in the first half of 2011, there has been a rather dramatic dip in the number of cases. So we have only had six this year. So the question before the committee and, in fact, before the Nation is: Was 2009 and 2010 sort of an outlier, or was it part of a pattern? I think that is still very much an open question, but we have seen some good news this year.

Thank you very much, Mr. Chairman.

Chairman KING. Thank you, Mr. Bergen.

[The statement of Mr. Bergen follows:]

PREPARED STATEMENT OF PETER BERGEN

MAY 25, 2011

Chairman King, Ranking Member Thompson, distinguished Members of the committee, thank you for the opportunity today to testify today about threats to the American homeland after the death of Osama bin Laden.

The death of bin Laden is devastating to "core" al-Qaeda, but arguably just as important to undermining the terrorist organization is the large amount of information that was recovered at the compound where he was killed in northern Pakistan on May 2, 2011. That information is already being exploited for leads. Between the "Arab Spring" and the death of bin Laden, both al-Qaeda's ideology and organization are under assault. That said, jihadist terrorism isn't going away. Regional affiliates such as al-Qaeda in the Arabian Peninsula remain threatening and there is a continued low-level threat posed by "homegrown" jihadist militants inspired by bin Laden's ideas.

Such militants might successfully carry out bombings against symbolic targets that would kill dozens, such as against subways in Manhattan, as was the plan in September 2009 of Najibullah Zazi, an Afghan-American al-Qaeda recruit, or they might blow up an American passenger jet, as was the intention 3 months later of the Nigerian Umar Farouq Abdulmutallab, who had been recruited by al-Qaeda in the Arabian Peninsula. Had that bombing attempt succeeded, it would have killed hundreds. This level of threat is likely to persist for years to come. However, al-Qaeda no longer poses a National security threat to the American homeland of the type that could result in a mass-casualty attack anywhere close to the scale of 9/11.

Indeed, a survey of the 180 individuals indicted or convicted in Islamist terrorism cases in the United States since the 9/11 attacks by the Maxwell School at Syracuse University and the New America Foundation found that none of the cases involved the use of chemical, biological, radiological, or nuclear weapons, while only four of the homegrown plots since 9/11 progressed to an actual attack in the United States, attacks that resulted in a total of 17 deaths. The most notable was the 2009 shootings at Ft. Hood, Texas by Maj. Nidal Malik Hasan, who killed 13. By way of comparison, according to the FBI, between 2001 and 2009, 73 people were killed in hate crimes in the United States.

The number of jihadist terrorism cases involving U.S. citizens or residents has markedly spiked in the past 2 years. In 2009 and 2010 there were 76, almost half of the total since 9/11, but in the first half of 2011 the number of such cases has subsided rather dramatically. This year there have been a total of just six jihadist terrorism cases by the date of this hearing.

American officials and the wider public should realize that by the law of averages al-Qaeda or an affiliate will succeed in getting some kind of attack through in the next years, and the best response to that would be to demonstrate that we as a society are resilient and are not be intimidated by such actions because our overreactions can play into the hands of the jihadist groups. When al-Qaeda or affiliated groups can provoke overwrought media coverage based on attacks that don't even succeed—such as the near-miss on Christmas day 2009 when Abdulmutallab tried to blow up Northwest Flight 253 over Detroit—we are doing their work for them. The person who best understood the benefits of American overreaction was bin Laden himself, who in 2004 said on a tape that aired on Al Jazeera: "All that we have to do is to send two mujahedeen to the furthest point east to raise a piece of cloth on which is written al-Qaeda, in order to make generals race there to cause America to suffer human, economic, and political losses."[1] Let us not give bin Laden any more such victories now that he is dead.

This testimony focuses on the threat from al-Qaeda, its affiliates, and those motivated by its ideas, while recognizing that these are not the only sources of terrorism directed against the United States.

The testimony will attempt to answer four questions:
- What effect will the killing of bin Laden have on U.S. security interests, and on core al-Qaeda's goals and capabilities?
- What threats emanate from Pakistan-based militant groups other than al-Qaeda?
- What threats emanate from al-Qaeda's regional affiliates?
- What threats emanate from domestic militants motivated by jihadist terrorist ideas?

1. What effect will the killing of bin Laden have on U.S. security interests, and on core al-Qaeda's goals and capabilities?

After the fall of the Taliban in the winter of 2001 bin Laden didn't, of course, continue to exert day-to-day control over al-Qaeda, but statements from him have always been the most reliable guide to the future actions of jihadist movements around the world and this remained the case even while he was on the run. In the past decade bin Laden issued more than 30 video- and audiotapes.[2] Those messages reached untold millions worldwide via television, the internet, and newspapers. The tapes not only instructed al-Qaeda's followers to continue to kill Westerners and Jews; some also carried specific instructions that militant cells then acted on. In

---

[1] Osama bin Laden, tape released November 1, 2004, *http://articles.cnn.com/2004-11-01/world/binladen.tape_1_al-jazeera-qaeda-bin?_s=PM:WORLD.*
[2] IntelCenter, a U.S. Government contractor that tracks jihadist publications, says bin Laden released 33 tapes in the 8 years between 9/11 and January 2010. IntelCenter Breakout of as-Sahab audio/video, 2002–26 February 2010. Email from Ben Venzke, February 26, 2010.

2003, bin Laden called for attacks against members of the coalition in Iraq; subsequently terrorists bombed commuters on their way to work in Madrid and London. Bin Laden also called for attacks on the Pakistani state in 2007, which is one of the reasons that Pakistan had more than 50 suicide attacks that year.[3] In March 2008 bin Laden denounced the publication of cartoons of the Prophet Mohammed in a Danish newspaper, which he said would soon be avenged. Three months later, an al-Qaeda suicide attacker bombed the Danish Embassy in Islamabad, killing six.

Bin Laden exercised near-total control over al-Qaeda, whose members had to swear a religious oath personally to bin Laden, so ensuring blind loyalty to him. Khalid Sheikh Mohammed, the operational commander of the 9/11 attacks, outlined the dictatorial powers that bin Laden exercised over his organization: "If the Shura council at al-Qaeda, the highest authority in the organization, had a majority of 98 percent on a resolution and it is opposed by bin Laden, he has the right to cancel the resolution."[4] Bin Laden's son Omar recalls that the men who worked for al-Qaeda had a habit of requesting permission before they spoke with their leader, saying, "Dear prince: May I speak?"[5] Materials recovered from the Abbottabad compound in northern Pakistan where bin Laden was killed paint a picture of a leader deeply involved in tactical, operational, and strategic planning for al-Qaeda, and in communication with other leaders of the group and even the organization's affiliates overseas.[6] The death of bin Laden eliminates the founder of al-Qaeda, which has only enjoyed one leader since its founding in 1988, and it also eliminates the one man who provided broad, largely unquestioned strategic goals to the wider jihadist movement. Around the world, those who joined al-Qaeda in the past two decades have sworn baya, a religious oath of allegiance to bin Laden, rather than to the organization itself, in the same way that Nazi party members swore an oath of fealty to Hitler, rather than to Nazism. That baya must now be transferred to whomever the new leader of al-Qaeda is going to be.

Of course, even as the al-Qaeda organization withers there are pretenders to bin Laden's throne. The first is the dour Egyptian surgeon, Ayman al-Zawahiri, who is the deputy leader of al-Qaeda, and therefore technically bin Laden's successor. But Zawahiri is not regarded as a natural leader and even among his fellow Egyptian militants Zawahiri is seen as a divisive force and so he is unlikely to be able to step into the role of the paramount leader of al-Qaeda and of the global jihadist movement that was occupied by bin Laden.[7] There is scant evidence that Zawahiri has the charisma of bin Laden, nor that he commands the respect bordering on love that was accorded to bin Laden by members of al-Qaeda.

Another possible leader of al-Qaeda is Saif al-Adel, also an Egyptian, who has played a role as a military commander of the terrorist group, and since 9/11 has spent many years living in Iran under some form of house arrest. Adel has been appointed the "caretaker" leader of the terrorist organization, according to Noman Benotman, a former leader of the Libyan Islamic Fighting Group, a militant organization that was once aligned with al-Qaeda, but has in recent years has renounced al-Qaeda's ideology.[8]

Benotman, who has known the leaders of al-Qaeda for more than two decades and has long been a reliable source of information about the inner workings of the terrorist group, says that based on his personal communications with militants and discussions on jihadist forums, Adel has emerged as the interim leader of al-Qaeda as it reels from the death of its founder and eventually transitions, presumably, to the uncharismatic Zawahiri.

[3] "Istanbul rocked by double bombing," BBC News, November 20, 2003, http://news.bbc.co.uk/2/hi/europe/3222608.stm; Craig Whitlock and Susan Glasser, "On tape, bin Laden tries new approach," Washington Post, December 17, 2004. http://www.washingtonpost.com/wp-dyn/articles/A3927-2004Dec16.html; Joel Roberts, "Al-Qaeda threatens more oil attacks," CBS News, February 25, 2006, http://www.cbsnews.com/stories/2006/02/27/world/main1346541_page2.shtml; "Bin Laden tape encourages Pakistanis to rebel," Associated Press, September 20, 2007, http://www.usatoday.com/news/world/2007-09-20-al-Qaeda-video_N.htm.
[4] Substitution for the testimony of KSM, trial of Zacarias Moussaoui, http://en.wikisource.org/wiki/Substitution_for_the_Testimony_of_KSM.
[5] Jean Sasson and Omar and Najwa bin Laden, Growing Up Bin Laden (St. Martin's Press: New York, NY, 2009), p. 161 and 213.
[6] Mark Mazzetti and Scott Shane, "Data show bin Laden plots," New York Times, May 5, 2011, http://www.nytimes.com/2011/05/06/world/asia/06intel.html.
[7] Jamal Ismail, interview by author, July 29, 2004, Islamabad, Pakistan.
[8] Peter Bergen, "Egyptian Saif al-Adel now acting leader of al-Qaeda," CNN.com, May 17, 2011, http://articles.cnn.com/2011-05-17/world/mideast.al.qaeda.appointee_1_al-adel-al-qaeda-libyan-islamic-fighting-group?_s=PM:WORLD.

A wild card is that one of bin Laden's dozen or so sons—endowed with an iconic family name—could eventually rise to take over the terrorist group. Already Saad bin Laden, one of the oldest sons, has played a middle management role in al-Qaeda.[9]

One of the key issues that any future leader of al-Qaeda has to reckon with now is dealing with the fallout from the large quantities of sensitive information that were recovered by U.S. forces at the compound in Abbottabad where bin Laden was killed. That information is likely to prove quite damaging to al-Qaeda's operations.

Jihadist terrorism will not, of course, disappear because of the death of bin Laden. Indeed, the Pakistan Taliban have already mounted attacks in Pakistan that they said were revenge for bin Laden's death,[10] but it is hard to imagine two more final endings to the "War on Terror" than the popular revolts against the authoritarian regimes in the Middle East and the death of bin Laden. No protestors in the streets of Cairo or Benghazi carried placards of bin Laden's face, and very few demanded the imposition of Taliban-like rule, al-Qaeda's preferred end-state for the countries in the region.

If the Arab Spring was a large nail in the coffin of al-Qaeda's ideology, the death of bin Laden was an equally large nail in the coffin of al-Qaeda the organization.

Media stories asserting that al-Qaeda has played no role in the revolts in the Middle East provoked a furious response from the Yemeni-American cleric Anwar al-Awlaki, a leader of Al-Qaeda in the Arabian Peninsula. In his group's *Inspire* magazine, a slick Web-based publication, heavy on photographs and graphics that, unusually for a jihadist organ, is written in colloquial English, Awlaki penned an essay titled "The Tsunami of Change." In the article, Awlaki made the uncontroversial point that the regimes based on fear were ending in the Arab world because of the revolutions and protests from Egypt to Bahrain. But he went on to assert that, contrary to commentators who had written that the Arab revolts represented a total repudiation of al-Qaeda's founding ideology, the world should "know very well that the opposite is the case."[11]

Awlaki also turned to this analyst, writing, "for a so-called 'terrorism expert' such as Peter Bergen, it is interesting to see how even he doesn't get it right this time. For him to think that because a Taliban-style regime is not going to take over following the revolutions, is a too short-term way of viewing the unfolding events." In other words: Just you wait—Taliban-type theocracies will be coming to the Middle East as the revolutions there unfold further. Awlaki also wrote that it was wrong to say that al-Qaeda viewed the revolutions in the Middle East with "despair." Instead, he claimed that "the Mujahedeen (holy warriors) around the world are going through a moment of elation and I wonder whether the West is aware of the upsurge in Mujahedeen activity in Egypt, Tunisia, Libya, Yemen, Arabia, Algeria and Morocco?"

We do not, of course, know the final outcome of the Arab revolutions, but there is very little chance that al-Qaeda or other extremist groups will be able to grab the reins of power as the authoritarian regimes of the Middle East crumble. But while al-Qaeda and its allies cannot take power anywhere in the Muslim world, these groups do thrive on chaos and civil war. And the whole point of revolutions is that they are inherently unpredictable even to the people who are leading them, so anything could happen in the coming years in Libya and Yemen, and much is unpredictable in Egypt, and even in Saudi Arabia.

2. What threats emanate from Pakistan-based militant groups other than al-Qaeda?

One of bin Laden's most toxic legacies is that even terrorist groups that don't call themselves "al-Qaeda" have adopted his ideology and a number of South Asian groups now threaten the West. According to Spanish prosecutors, the late leader of the Pakistani Taliban, Baitullah Mehsud sent a team of would-be suicide bombers to Barcelona to attack the subway system there in January 2008. A Pakistani Taliban spokesman confirmed this in a videotaped interview in which he said that

[9] Douglas Farah and Dana Priest, "Bin Laden son plays key role in al-Qaeda," *Washington Post,* October 14, 2003, *http://www.washingtonpost.com/wp-dyn/content/article/2007/08/20/AR2007082000980.html.*

[10] Reza Sayah, "Blasts kill at least 70 in northwest Pakistan," CNN.com, May 12, 2011, *http://articles.cnn.com/2011-05-12/world/pakistan.explosions_1_drone-strikes-north-waziristan-militants?_s=PM:WORLD.*

[11] Anwar al-Awlaki, "Tsunami of change," *Inspire,* March 2011, *http://info.publicintelligence.net/InspireMarch2011.pdf.*

24

those suicide bombers "were under pledge to Baitullah Mehsud" and were sent because of the Spanish military presence in Afghanistan.[12]

In 2009 the Pakistani Taliban trained an American recruit for an attack in New York. Faisal Shahzad, who had once worked as a financial analyst in the accounting department at the Elizabeth Arden cosmetics company in Stamford, Connecticut, travelled to Pakistan where he received 5 days of bomb-making training from the Taliban in the tribal region of Waziristan. Armed with this training and $12,000 in cash, Shahzad returned to Connecticut where he purchased a Nissan Pathfinder. He placed a bomb in the SUV and detonated it in Times Square on May 1, 2010 around 6 p.m. when the sidewalks were thick with tourists and theatergoers. The bomb, which was designed to act as a fuel-air explosive, luckily was a dud and Shahzad was arrested 2 days later as he tried to leave JFK airport for Dubai.[13]

Also based in the Pakistani tribal regions are a number of other jihadist groups allied to both the Taliban and al-Qaeda such as the such as the Islamic Movement of Uzbekistan and the Islamic Jihad Union that have trained dozens of Germans for attacks in Europe. Two Germans and a Turkish resident in Germany, for instance, trained in the tribal regions and then planned to bomb the massive U.S. Ramstein airbase in Germany in 2007.[14] Before their arrests, the men had obtained 1,600 pounds of industrial strength hydrogen peroxide, enough to make a number of large bombs.[15]

The Mumbai attacks of 2008 showed that bin Laden's ideas about attacking Western and Jewish targets had also spread to Pakistani militant groups such as Lashkar-e-Taiba (LeT), which had previously focused only on Indian targets. Over a 3-day period in late November 2008 LeT carried out multiple attacks in Mumbai targeting five-star hotels housing Westerners and a Jewish-American community center. The Pakistani-American David Headley played a key role in LeT's massacre in Mumbai traveling to the Indian financial capital on five extended trips in the 2 years before the attacks. There Headley made videotapes of the key locations attacked by the ten LeT gunmen including the Taj Mahal and Oberoi hotels and Chabad House, the Jewish community center.[16]

Sometime in 2008, Headley hatched a plan to attack the Danish newspaper *Jyllands-Posten,* which 3 years earlier had published cartoons of the Prophet Mohammed that were deemed to be offensive by many Muslims. In January 2009 Headley traveled to Copenhagen, where he reconnoitered the *Jyllands-Posten* newspaper on the pretext that he ran an immigration business that was looking to place some advertising in the paper. Following his trip to Denmark, Headley met with Ilyas Kashmiri in the Pakistani tribal regions to brief him on his findings. Kashmiri ran a terrorist organization, Harakat-ul-Jihad Islami, closely tied to al-Qaeda. Headley returned to Chicago in mid-June 2009 and was arrested there 3 months later as he was preparing to leave for Pakistan again. He told investigators that he was planning to kill the *Jyllands-Posten's* cultural editor who had first commissioned the cartoons as well as the cartoonist Kurt Westergaard who had drawn the cartoon he found most offensive; the Prophet Mohammed with a bomb concealed in his turban.[17]

The Pakistani Taliban, Lashkar-e-Taiba, Harakat-ul-Jihad Islami, the Islamic Jihad Union and the Islamic Movement of Uzbekistan are all based or have a significant presence in Pakistan's tribal regions and have track records of trying to attack Western and/or American targets and should therefore all be considered threats to American interests. The Pakistani Taliban, Lashkar-e-Taiba and Harakat-ul-Jihad Islami have also been able to attract American recruits. Already the Pakistani Taliban has carried out attacks in response to bin Laden's death.[18]

---

[12] Fernando Reinares, "A case study of the January 2008 suicide bomb plot in Barcelona," Combating Terrorism Center Sentinel, January 15, 2009, *http://www.ctc.usma.edu/posts/a-case-study-of-the-january-2008-suicide-bomb-plot-in-barcelona.*

[13] Benjamin Weiser and Colin Moynihan, "Guilty plea in Times Square bomb plot," *New York Times,* June 21, 2010, *http://www.nytimes.com/2010/06/22/nyregion/22terror.html.*

[14] Paul Cruickshank, "The Militant Pipeline," New America Foundation, February 2010, *http://counterterrorism.newamerica.net/sites/newamerica.net/files/policydocs/cruickshank.pdf.*

[15] "Four jailed over plot to attack U.S. bases," Associated Press, Stamford 4, 2010, *http://www.msnbc.msn.com/id/35702791/ns/world__news-europe/t/four-jailed-over-plot-attack-us-bases/.*

[16] *USA* v. *David Coleman Headley*, U.S. District Court Northern District of Illinois Eastern Division Case No. 09 CR 830.

[17] Sebastian Rotella, "Pakistan's terror connections," ProPublica, *http://www.propublica.org/topic/mumbai-terror-attacks/.*

[18] Reza Sayah, "Blasts kill at least 70 in northwest Pakistan," CNN.com, May 12, 2011, *http://articles.cnn.com/2011-05-12/world/pakistan.explosions__1__drone-strikes-north-waziristan-militants?_s=PM:WORLD.*

3. WHAT THREATS EMANATE FROM AL-QAEDA'S REGIONAL AFFILIATES?

Al-Qaeda in the Arabian Peninsula (AQAP)

Anwar al-Awlaki, the American-born cleric living in Yemen has increasingly taken an operational role in "al-Qaeda in the Arabian Peninsula," (AQAP) which was responsible for attempting to bring down Northwest Flight 253 over Detroit on Christmas day 2009 with a bomb secreted in the underwear of Umar Farouk Abdulmutallab, a Nigerian recruit. If Abdulmutallab had succeeded in bringing down the passenger jet, the bombing not only would have killed hundreds but would also have had a large effect on the U.S. economy already reeling from the effect of the worst recession since the Great Depression, and would have devastated the critical aviation and tourism businesses.

President Obama regards Awlaki as so dangerous that he has authorized, seemingly for the first time in American history, the assassination of a U.S. citizen. Awlaki's command of English and internet savvy helped to radicalize militants such as Major Nidal Hasan who killed 13 of his fellow soldiers at Ft. Hood Texas in 2009. That attack happened after a series of email exchanges between Hasan and Awlaki in which the cleric said it was religiously sanctioned for Hasan to kill fellow soldiers.[19]

In October 2010 AQAP hid bombs in toner cartridges on planes bound for Chicago that were only discovered at the last moment at East Midlands Airport and in Dubai.[20] The skillful AQAP bomb-maker who made those bombs is still at large, according to U.S. officials and will continue to attempt to smuggle hard-to-detect bombs on to American or other Western planes.

While carrying out bin Laden's overall strategy of attacking the United States, AQAP was operating largely independent of him and so will not be much affected by bin Laden's death.

Al Shabab

In September 2009, the Somali Islamist insurgent group Al Shabab ("the youth" in Arabic) formally pledged allegiance to bin Laden following a 2-year period in which it had recruited Somali-Americans and other U.S. Muslims to fight in the war in Somalia.[21] Six months earlier bin Laden had given his imprimatur to the Somali jihad in an audiotape released titled "Fight On, Champions of Somalia."[22] After it announced its fealty to bin Laden, Shabab was able to recruit larger numbers of foreign fighters, by one estimate up to 1,200 were working with the group by 2010. Today, Shabab controls much of southern Somalia.[23] Worrisomely, Shabab has shown an ability to send its operatives outside of Somalia, killing dozens in suicide attacks in Uganda last year[24] and dispatching an assassin to Denmark to kill Kurt Westergaard, the Danish cartoonist who had drawn the cartoons of the Prophet Mohamed that were deemed to be offensive. The cartoonist only survived the assault because he had taken the precaution of installing a safe room in his house.[25]

Shabab has managed to plant al-Qaeda-like ideas into the heads of even its American recruits. Shirwa Ahmed, an ethnic Somali, graduated from high school in Minneapolis in 2003, and then worked pushing passengers in wheelchairs at Minneapolis Airport. In late 2007 Ahmed traveled to Somalia and a year later, on October 29, 2008, Ahmed drove a truck loaded with explosives towards a government compound in Puntland, northern Somalia, blowing himself up and killing about 20 people. The FBI matched Ahmed's finger, recovered at the scene of the bombing, to

[19] Brian Ross, "Major Hasan's email: 'I can't wait to join you' in the afterlife," ABC, November 19, 2009, *http://abcnews.go.com/Blotter/major-hasans-mail-wait-join-afterlife/story?id=9130339*.

[20] Scott Shane, "U.S. hunts for more suspicious packages," *New York Times*, October 30, 2010, *http://www.nytimes.com/2010/10/31/us/31plane.html*.

[21] Agence France Presse, "Somalia's al-Shabab proclaims allegiance to al-Qaeda chief," September 23, 2009.

[22] Osama bin Laden, "Fight on, champions of Somalia," March 19, 2009, *http://www.nefafoundation.org/miscellaneous/nefaubl0309-2.pdf*.

[23] BBC News, "Somalia: government captures al-Shabab militia bases," March 5, 2011, *http://www.bbc.co.uk/news/world-africa-12657466*.

[24] Sudarsan Raghavan, "Islamic militant group al-Shabab claims Uganda bombing," *Washington Post*, July 12, 2010, *http://www.washingtonpost.com/wp-dyn/content/article/2010/07/12/AR2010071200476.html*.

[25] BBC News, "Danish police shoot intruder at cartoonist's home," January 2, 2010, *http://news.bbc.co.uk/2/hi/8437433.stm*.

fingerprints already on file for him. Ahmed was the first American suicide attacker anywhere.[26]

Given the high death rate for the Americans fighting in Somalia, as well as the considerable attention this group has received from the FBI, it is unlikely that the couple of dozen American veterans of the Somali war pose much of a threat to the United States itself. It is however, plausible now that Shabab had declared itself to be an al-Qaeda affiliate, that U.S. citizens in the group might be recruited to engage in anti-American operations overseas.

Shabab has operated independently of al-Qaeda "core" and so will not be much affected by bin Laden's death.

Al-Qaeda in Iraq (AQI)

In 2008 there was a sense that al-Qaeda in Iraq (AQI) was on the verge of defeat. The American ambassador to Iraq, Ryan Crocker said, "You are not going to hear me say that al-Qaeda is defeated, but they've never been closer to defeat than they are now."[27] Certainly AQI has lost its ability to control large swaths of the country and a good chunk of the Sunni population as it did in 2006, but the group has proven surprisingly resilient as demonstrated by the fact that it pulled off large-scale bombings in central Baghdad in 2010 and 2011. AQI has also shown some ability to carry out operations outside Iraq as well: It attacked three American hotels in Amman, Jordan in 2005[28] and it had some sort of role in the attacks on Glasgow Airport 2 years later.[29] As U.S. forces pull down in Iraq, AQI may be tempted to mount other out-of-country attacks against American or Western targets.

The death of bin Laden is unlikely to affect AQI much.

Al-Qaeda in the Islamic Maghreb (AQIM)

In September 2006 the Algerian Salafist Group for Preaching and Combat's leader Abu Musab Abdul Wadud, explained that al-Qaeda "is the only organization qualified to gather together the mujahideen." Subsequently taking the name "al-Qaeda in the Islamic Maghreb" (AQIM), the group, which had traditionally focused only on Algerian targets, conducted a range of operations: Bombing the United Nations building in Algiers; attacking the Israeli embassy in Mauritania; and murdering French and British hostages. AQIM has hitherto not been able to carry out attacks in the West and is one of the weakest of al-Qaeda's affiliates, only having the capacity for infrequent attacks in North Africa.[30]

4. WHAT THREATS EMANATE FROM DOMESTIC MILITANTS MOTIVATED BY JIHADIST TERRORIST IDEAS?

The New America Foundation and Syracuse University's Maxwell School of Public Policy examined the 180 post-9/11 cases of Americans or U.S. residents convicted or charged of some form of jihadist terrorist activity directed against the United States, as well as the cases of those American citizens who have traveled overseas to join a jihadist terrorist group.[32] None of the cases we investigated involved individuals plotting with chemical, biological, radiological, or nuclear weapons. Given all the post-9/11 concerns about terrorists armed with weapons of mass destruction this is one of our more positive findings.

The number of jihadist terrorism cases involving U.S. citizens or residents has spiked in the past 2 years.[33] In 2009 and 2010 there were 76, almost half of the

[26] Spencer Hsu and Carrie Johnson, "Somali Americans recruited by extremists," *Washington Post,* March 11, 2009, *http://www.washingtonpost.com/wp-dyn/content/article/2009/03/10/AR2009031003901.html;* "Joining the fight in Somalia," *New York Times,* interactive timeline, July 12, 2009, *http://www.nytimes.com/interactive/2009/07/12/us/20090712-somalia-timeline.html.*
[27] Lee Keath, "Al Qaeda is close to defeat in Iraq, U.S. ambassador says," Associated Press, May 25, 2008, *http://www.boston.com/news/world/articles/2008/05/25/al_qaeda_is_close_to_defeat_in_iraq_us_ambassador_says/?comments=all.*
[28] BBC News, "Al-Qaeda claims Jordan attacks," November 10, 2005, *http://news.bbc.co.uk/2/hi/4423714.stm.*
[29] Raymond Bonner, Jane Perlez, and Eric Schmitt, "British inquiry of jailed plot points to Iraq's Qaeda group," *New York Times,* December 14, 2007, *http://www.nytimes.com/2007/12/14/world/europe/14london.html.*
[31] Quoted in Peter Bergen, "Where you bin?" The New Republic, *January 29, 2006.*
[32] Peter Bergen, Andrew Lebovich, Matthew Reed, Laura Hohnsbeen, Nicole Salter, and Sophie Schmidt at the New America Foundation, and Professor William Banks, Alyssa Procopio, Jason Cherish, Joseph Robertson, Matthew Michaelis, Richard Lim, Laura Adams, and Drew Dickinson from the Maxwell School at Syracuse University all worked on creating this database, which is available at *http://homegrown.newamerica.net.*
[33] Note: From our count we excluded post-9/11 cases in the United States involving either Hezbollah or Hamas as neither group has targeted Americans since 9/11. We did include groups

total since 9/11. This increase was driven, in part, by plots that could have killed dozens, such as the Pakistani-American Faisal Shahzad's attempt to bomb Times Square in May 2010, but also by the 31 people who were charged with fundraising, recruiting, or traveling abroad to fight for the Somali terrorist group, Al-Shabab.

In 2002 there were 16 jihadist terrorism cases, in 2003 there were 23, in 2004 there were 8, in 2005 there were 12, in 2006 there were 18, in 2007 there were 16, in 2008 there were 5, in 2009 there were a record 43, in 2010 there were 33, and in 2011 the number of such cases has subsided rather dramatically: There were 6.

The total number of deaths from jihadist-terrorist attacks in the United States after 9/11 totals 17. Maj. Nidal Malik Hasan is accused of opening fire at a readiness center at Fort Hood, Texas in 2009, killing 13; Hesham Mohamed Hadayat killed two people at the El Al counter at Los Angeles International Airport in 2002 before being shot dead by an El Al security guard; Naveed Haq was found guilty of killing one person at a Jewish center in Seattle in 2006; and Carlos Bledsoe (aka Abdulhakim Mujahid Muhammed) is accused of killing one soldier and wounding another at a U.S. Army recruiting center in Arkansas in 2009.

The U.S. military, fighting wars of various kinds in five Muslim countries, is firmly in the crosshairs of homegrown jihadist militants. Around one in three of the cases examined by the Maxwell School and New America involved a U.S. military target, ranging from Quantico Marine Base in Virginia to American soldiers serving overseas. We found 57 individuals who were targeting U.S. military facilities or personnel both at home and abroad; 35% of the cases. Bryant Neal Vinas, for instance, a Long Island native admitted in 2009 to taking part in a rocket attack on a U.S. base in Afghanistan, while in North Carolina Daniel Boyd, a charismatic convert to Islam who had fought in the jihad in Afghanistan against the Soviets, had some kind of plan to attack American soldiers. Boyd obtained maps of Quantico Marine Base in Virginia, which he cased for a possible attack on June 12, 2009.[34]

Rather than being the uneducated, young Arab-American immigrants of popular imagination, the homegrown militants do not fit any particular socio-economic or ethnic profile. Their average age is 30. Of the cases for which ethnicity could be determined, only a quarter are of Arab descent, while 10% are African-American, 13% are Caucasian, 18% are South Asian, 20% are of Somali descent, and the rest are either mixed race or of other ethnicities. About half the cases involved a U.S-born American citizen, while another third were naturalized citizens. And of the 94 cases where education could be ascertained, two-thirds pursued at least some college courses, and 1 in 10 had completed a Masters, PhD, or doctoral equivalent.

Chairman KING. Our next witness is Evan Kohlmann. He has served as an expert witness on al-Qaeda for the Department of Defense in the military commission proceedings. He is an international terrorism consultant. He has authored "Al Qaeda's Jihad in Europe". He is the founder and senior partner at Flashpoint Global Partners, a New York-based security consulting firm, and appears on television as a terrorism analyst.

Mr. Kohlmann, I welcome you to the committee for the first time and look forward to your testimony.

STATEMENT OF EVAN F. KOHLMANN, FLASHPOINT GLOBAL PARTNERS

Mr. KOHLMANN. Thank you very much, Mr. Chairman. Thank you also, Ranking Member Thompson and the rest of the committee, for having me here today.

I would like to start off with kind of beginning at the very beginning. Over the last decade, one of the central pillars of U.S. counterterrorism policy has been to aggressively target al-Qaeda

---

allied to al-Qaeda such as the Somali group Al-Shabab, or that are influenced by al-Qaeda's ideology such as the Pakistani group Lashkar-e-Taiba, which sought out and killed Americans in the Mumbai attacks of 2008. We also included individuals motivated by al-Qaeda's ideology of violence directed at the United States.

[34] *USA v Daniel Patrick Boyd et al.* Indictment in U.S. District Court for the Eastern District of North Carolina, filed 7/22/09 *http://www.investigativeproject.org/documents/case_docs/1029.pdf;* and the superseding indictment in the same case dated September 24, 2009. *http://www.investigativeproject.org/documents/case_docs/1075.pdf.*

leadership—as you can see right there—in their long-time sanctuary regions in Afghanistan and Pakistan. As President Obama
explained on television in 2009, this is the heart of it. This is where
bin Laden is. It is from here you see attacks launched not just
against the United States, but against London, against Bali,
against a whole host of countries.

On May 1, that mission culminated in the now successful killing
of bin Laden at a hideout in Abbottabad. Were we still stuck in October 2001, this might be the end of the narrative; however, much
has changed in the world since those early days of the battle
against al-Qaeda. The gaps in al-Qaeda's central leadership created
by the deaths of former al-Qaeda military chief Abu Hafs al-Masri
and other luminaries have been filled by new, younger figures.

With the blessings of bin Laden and Ayman al-Zawahiri, regional
al-Qaeda leaderships have emerged in critical locations such as
Iraq, Saudi Arabia, Yemen, and North Africa. Meanwhile, a new
generation of home-grown lone wolf-style jihadists has emerged, including many U.S. and European nationals who may lack the military skills to plan the next 9/11, but whose passion for violence and
bloodshed can nonetheless have deadly consequences.

To understand what the future of al-Qaeda will now be, one must
first assess the immediate reactions to the death of their revered
former leader among its most diehard supporters, and what becomes obvious from the internal discussions taking place right now
is that the sudden word of bin Laden's death came as a nasty shock
to his followers. One of the most disturbing parts of all this was
the wealth of intelligence that was recovered from bin Laden's compound in Abbottabad. One of the most credible and respected users
on al-Qaeda's top-tier "Shamukh" discussion forum, Yaman
Mukhadab, posted a warning advising that these are "the most
dangerous 72 hours in the struggle of al-Qaeda with the Zionists
and Crusaders in the history of the jihadi struggle." He cautioned,
"It is possible that America has infiltrated Mujahideen communications and will seek to unveil the masterminds behind big terrorist
operations."

As far as I see it, any group of Mujahideen that are assigned to
an operation should go forward and execute it without hesitation
or delay and to avoid completely attempting to communicate with
anyone.

Unfortunately, the sense of melancholy and panic that was brewing in the hearts of al-Qaeda supporters and followers was soon
swamped by a tidal wave of rage, especially after images of crowds
of jubilant Americans were televised around the world as they cele-
brated at Ground Zero and outside of the White House.

One user on another al-Qaeda web forum, Ta'er Muhajir, posted
an open message addressed to "You who danced in front of the
White House, we, too, will start to dance the next time we hear
about a massacre that befalls you, just as we danced when your
corpses were spread across the Pentagon and the World Trade Center."

In another message titled, "Advice and Guidance for the Lions
Launching Attacks in the Land of America." Another user,
Azmarai, explained, "We aren't merely seeking to kill a soldier or
an American civilian here or there, as this doesn't change any-

thing. Our goal is bigger than that. Like our Sheikh Osama ordered us in his messages, it is critical to continue jihadi operations both against the United States military and economy. Their economic destruction is on-going, but it requires more attacks and for the young men to strike at the strategic points of the American economy."

I now turn to the issue of al-Qaeda's remaining central leadership figures. You will see a chart up there of those who are still left post the death of bin Laden. Of course, with bin Laden now gone, the question naturally turns to who will be selected to replace his now vacant position as the overall commander of al-Qaeda. Though the identity of that leader—that new leader—remains still uncertain, the far most likely candidate, as indicated on the chart here, is al-Qaeda's present deputy commander, Dr. Ayman al-Zawahiri. Al-Zawahiri, who merged his Egyptian Islamic Jihad faction with al-Qaeda in 1998, has long stood alongside bin Laden as his closest adviser. Al-Zawahiri has both played a key role in operationally organizing and overseeing international terrorist attacks and has also simultaneously spearheaded al-Qaeda media efforts.

As far as supporters chatting on top-tier al-Qaeda web forums, there simply has been no serious discussion of any potential bin Laden successors other than Dr. Ayman al-Zawahiri. Al-Qaeda's on-line constituents are so taken with the idea that al-Zawahiri will be the next leader of al-Qaeda that they have taken to casually referring to the group as Jund Ayman, or the Soldiers of Ayman. Forum user Muheb Ruyat al-Rahman insisted, our Sheikh Mohammad, may Allah have mercy on him, is our Sheikh Ayman. Our Sheikh Ayman is our Sheikh Osama.

There is also the question of al-Qaeda's regional affiliates faced with the resounding defeat on the peaks of Tora Bora in late 2001. A group of high-ranking al-Qaeda commanders decided to embrace the development of a more diffuse and self-sufficient network of international operatives. Al-Qaeda's beneficial website acknowledged that it was time for a new phase in evolution. "The al-Qaeda organization has adopted a strategy in its war with the Americans based on expanding the battlefield and exhausting the enemy. The more diversified and distant the areas in which the operations take place, the more exhausting it becomes for the enemy, the more he needs to stretch his resources, and the more he becomes terrified."

By mid-2004, nascent al-Qaeda franchise organizations were already well ensconced in both Saudi Arabia and Iraq. Today similar al-Qaeda franchises have expanded their reach even farther, into Indonesia, Yemen, Algeria, Somalia, Lebanon, and the Palestinian territories. These upstart regional branches are capable of operating basically independently of al-Qaeda's central leadership in Afghanistan. The growing affiliate factions often have more expansive ambitions or just as grandiose as those of bin Laden himself.

While al-Qaeda's regional efforts in Iraq and Saudi Arabia may have suffered debilitating setbacks in recent years, that is not the case in Yemen, where a growing al-Qaeda branch, known as al-Qaeda in the Arabian Peninsula, has demonstrated its ability to launch repeated and sophisticated attacks targeting U.S. soil.

Perhaps the most disturbing aspects of launching attacks against the United States is their obsession with conceiving plots aimed at causing catastrophic damage to the American economy. In early 2008, AQAP published an approving interview with a most wanted al-Qaeda suspect, who endorsed the idea of striking at oil resources, petroleum resources. He explained if the enemy's interests in the Arabian Peninsula were stricken, and a supply of oil was cut off, and the oil refineries were out of order, this would cause the enemy to collapse, and he won't merely withdraw from Iraq and Afghanistan, but he would face total collapse. If he were struck hard from various places, then he would scatter and turn around and flee forlornly from the land of the Muslims.

Given the high-profile role that AQAP has played in masterminding not only the underwear bomber, Omar Abdulmutallab, but also most recently a cargo bomb plot aimed at the United States, AQAP's passionate interest in launching strategic attacks aimed at devastating the U.S. economy can be ignored only at our own peril. It is also a telling reminder of how, thanks to the new affiliate network of global franchises, the underlying al-Qaeda terrorist threat to the U.S. homeland is in some ways unchanged by the death of Osama bin Laden.

Thank you very much.

[The statement of Mr. Kohlmann follows:]

PREPARED STATEMENT OF EVAN F. KOHLMANN WITH LAITH ALKHOURI

MAY 25, 2011

(I) INTRODUCTION

Over the last decade, one of the central pillars of U.S. counterterrorism policy has been to aggressively target al-Qaeda's senior leadership in their long-time sanctuary in regions in Afghanistan and Pakistan. The prevailing wisdom behind this strategy is quite simple: By mounting direct pressure on Osama bin Laden, Ayman al-Zawahiri, and others within the highest echelons, al-Qaeda will presumably lack the time, resources, and opportunity to conceive complex international terrorist plots threatening U.S. homeland security. As President Obama explained in 2009 during a televised interview, "This is the heart of it. This is where bin Laden is. This is where [his] allies are. It's from here that you see attacks launched not just against the United States, but against London, against Bali, against a whole host of countries." Indeed, the American government has invested billions of dollars and tens of thousands of U.S. soldiers in order to carry out this mission and deny al-Qaeda the use of a central base in South Asia. On May 1, the mission culminated in the successful killing of Osama bin Laden at a hideout in Abbottabad, Pakistan by a team of U.S. Navy SEALs. Evidence recovered by the SEALs reportedly shows that bin Laden continued to play a direct operational role in conceiving and micro-managing terrorist plots against the United States.

Were we still stuck in October 2001, this might be the end of the narrative for bin Laden's jihadi movement. However, much has indeed changed in the world since those early days of the battle against al-Qaeda. The gaps in al-Qaeda's central leadership created by the deaths of former luminaries like Abu Hafs al-Masri and Abu Laith al-Liby have been filled by new younger figures like Abu Yahya al-Liby. With the blessings of bin Laden and Ayman al-Zawahiri, regional al-Qaeda leaderships have emerged in critical locations such as Iraq, Saudi Arabia, Yemen, and North Africa. Meanwhile, a new generation of homegrown "lone wolf"-style jihadists has emerged (including many U.S. and European nationals) who may lack the military skills to plan the next 9/11, but whose passion for violence and bloodshed can nonetheless have deadly consequences.

(II) REACTION TO THE DEATH OF BIN LADEN

To understand what the future of al-Qaeda will now be, one must first assess the immediate reactions to the death of their revered former leader among its most diehard supporters. Late on the evening of May 1, al-Qaeda's on-line social networking forums were shaken awake in a spasm of activity as jihadi militants from around the globe rushed to log in and discover for themselves if reports of the killing of bin Laden were really true. With al-Qaeda's remaining leaders still hiding quietly out of sight for the time being, these on-line forums provide one of the most compelling available windows into the thinking of Bin Laden's cadre as they mourn his passing.

At first, the response was largely one of chaotic disbelief. Stunned forum participants insisted that the announcement had to be part of a new scheme devised by the CIA to trick and demoralize bin Laden's diehard supporters. With their patience quickly exhausted by the deluge of anxious incoming inquiries, ill-tempered forum administrators began threatening to permanently ban anyone who even dared to express sorrow based on "unverified crusader rumors" of bin Laden's demise. Finally, on May 6, al-Qaeda's central leadership issued a formal communiqué acknowledging bin Laden's "martyrdom." The message defiantly insisted, "Shaykh Usama didn't build an organization to die with it and go away with it . . . The university of faith, Quran, and jihad that was founded by Sheikh Usama bin Laden has not and will not close its doors . . . those of us from the al-Qaedat ul-Jihad network vow to Allah to continue on the path of jihad taken by our leaders, headed by Sheikh Usama, without hesitation or question, and we will not deviate or lean from that."[1]

What first becomes obvious from the discussions taking place on al-Qaeda's on-line chat forums is that—no matter what the organization's leadership may claim in retrospect—the sudden word of bin Laden's death came as a nasty shock to his followers, and was undoubtedly a staggering blow. In the hours immediately following news of bin Laden's violent demise, al-Qaeda forum users and administrators were also preoccupied with another gnawing concern: The state of their own personal security. By the morning after the raid, media sources were reporting that U.S. Navy SEALs had seized an intelligence jackpot of hard drives, flash data disks, and other records of electronic communications from the bin Laden compound in Abbottabad. One of the most credible and respected users on al-Qaeda's top-tier "Shamukh" web forum, "Yaman Mukhadab", posted a warning to fellow jihadists advising that these were "the most dangerous 72 hours in the struggle of al-Qaeda with the Zionists and Crusaders . . . in the history of the jihad struggle."[2] He cautioned, "it is possible that America has infiltrated mujahideen communications and will seek to unveil the masterminds behind big [terrorist] operations." He further urged, "As far as I see it, any group of mujahideen that are assigned to an operation should go forward and execute it . . . without hesitation or delay, and to completely avoid trying to communicate with anyone . . . or to seek new orders . . . Stopping and delaying while awaiting something new will not achieve anything, and it won't change what has already taken place."[3]

The palpable sense of melancholy and panic brewing in the hearts of al-Qaeda's supporters on the web was soon swamped by a tidal wave of raw, unbridled rage, especially after televised images of crowds of jubilant Americans celebrating outside the White House and at Ground Zero were broadcast around the world. One user, "Ta'er Muhajir", posted an open message on al-Qaeda's web forums addressed to "you who danced in front of the White House . . . We, too, will start to dance the next time we hear about a massacre that befalls you, just as we danced when your rotten corpses were spread across the Pentagon and the World Trade Center."[4] Another forum user, "Mukhadab ad-Dima" (a nickname which translates to "Drenched in Blood"), pointed to the "big crowds in front of the White House" and demanded, "who will be the hero who will turn their night into day and their morning into hell, and who will renew the September glories—who will follow next in the list of our heroes: Arid Uka, Faisal Shahzad, Umar Farouk Abdulmutallab, Nidal Hassan . . . ?"[5] Echoing this sentiment, jihadi forum user "Jaish al-Islam" scoffed, "they are celebrating the martyrdom of Shaykh Usama, but what they don't realize is that we are all Usama."[6]

Even as he acknowledged his "sadness over the loss of our Shaykh Usama Bin Laden", jihadi forum user "Abu al-Qassam al-Maqdisi" vowed to "continue on this path." Openly addressing U.S. President Barack Obama, he mocked, "if you think that by killing Shaykh Abu Abdullah you have finished off al-Qaeda, then you are totally delusional . . . the martyrdom of Shaykh Usama didn't weaken us and

[1] http://shamikh1.net/vb/showthread.php?t=108210. May 6, 2011.
[2] http://shamikh1.net/vb/showthread.php?t=107305. May 3, 2011.
[3] http://shamikh1.net/vb/showthread.php?t=107305. May 3, 2011.
[4] http://shamikh1.net/vb/showthread.php?t=107232. May 2, 2011.
[5] http://shamikh1.net/vb/showthread.php?t=107132. May 2, 2011.
[6] http://shamikh1.net/vb/showthread.php?t=107100&page=4. May 2, 2011

didn't disappoint us—it just gave us more passion to stay steadfast on this path. And if you have killed Usama, then we are all Usama."[7] These repeated declarations of defiance inevitably turned to the question of how best to avenge the "martyrdom" of bin Laden. Another registered user, "Abu Musab al-Maqdisi", complained, "unfortunately, the only thing I see is men who are crying over nothing . . . It would have been better to see the knife of Zarqawi being sharpened to the point that I can behold its shine from here."[8] He urged fellow bin Laden supporters, "Beware, and get ready. And I don't know if there is time to say goodbye to your fathers, mothers, wives, children, brothers and neighbors, as time can't wait and the Shaykh can't wait, and now the battle has begun to eradicate the state of infidels, America, and anyone who stands alongside it from within the Muslim lands. It's only a matter of hours. Ohhh, hours are too many, just minutes, and even too much . . . secondssss . . . I'm now sharpening my sword so you should be sharpening yours."[9]

Jihadi forum users have also been tendering their own unsolicited suggestions and insights to al-Qaeda's remaining leadership. In a message titled "Advice and Guidance for the Lions Launching Attacks in the Land of the Enemy, America", user "Azmarai" addressed "those who will be planning in the coming days, weeks, and months to carry out operations in the United States": "we aren't merely seeking to kill a soldier or an American civilian here or there, as this doesn't change anything . . . Our goal is bigger than that . . . Like our Shaykh Usama ordered us in his messages, it is critical to continue jihadi operations both against the U.S. military and economy . . . Their economic destruction is on-going, but it requires more attacks and for the young men to strike at the strategic points of the American economy." Towards the end of causing catastrophic damage to the U.S. economy, user "Azmarai" suggested a range of possible targets, including targeting hydroelectric dams, "major electricity-producing plants", nuclear power plants, oil refineries, "Federal Reserve Banks and major financial centers", and water-purification facilities. "Azmarai" was equally insistent on the need for al-Qaeda and its supporters to specifically "target the major companies that contribute technologically in supporting the U.S. army with information and technology, like the headquarters of DARPA . . . Killing America's scientists and those who participate in advancing military research is very important . . . Also target the headquarters of the big weapon manufacturing companies, and specifically targeting their main headquarters that include engineers and experts."[10]

Equally of note is a formal communiqué issued in response to bin Laden's death by the official team of on-line couriers responsible for distributing al-Qaeda's digital propaganda. The so-called "Fajr Media Center" included a direct "Message to the American People":

"We say to you: killing the Shaykh was a big mistake, and a great sin, and a deed that will bring catastrophes upon you that will sink your joy. Obama has sacrificed your blood to remain in his position of power . . . Obama is not different from his predecessor Bush in anything, as the wars Bush started Obama continued and he didn't do anything to stop them . . . Do not blame us after today; you elected him and you will pay the price! Armies may protect Obama, but who protects you from our reach?"[11]

Fajr Media Center also offered their own message of advice "for the Mujahideen", urging al-Qaeda supporters to exact a heavy price in revenge for the "martyrdom" of bin Laden—"the kind of revenge that will make America forget her present euphoria and instead scream with pain." Echoing the popular sentiments among jihadi forum users, the group advocated "every Muslim mujahid" should "focus on making suitable preparations for any operation against the infidels, and we encourage that the operations be unique, and terribly devastating to the enemy . . . If the chance comes up, do not waste it, and do not consult anyone in killing the Americans and destroying their economy. The land of Allah is wide and their interests are widespread . . . We encourage you to launch individual terrorist operations that reap major results but which require only basic preparations."[12]

[7] http://shamikh1.net/vb/showthread.php?t=107175. May 2, 2011.
[8] http://shamikh1.net/vb/showthread.php?t=107288. May 2, 2011.
[9] http://shamikh1.net/vb/showthread.php?t=107288. May 2, 2011.
[10] http://shamikh1.net/vb/showthread.php?t=109881. May 13, 2011.
[11] http://shamikh1.net/vb/showthread.php?t=109164. May 9, 2011.
[12] http://shamikh1.net/vb/showthread.php?t=109164. May 9, 2011.

(III) AL-QAEDA'S REMAINING CENTRAL LEADERSHIP FIGURES

It is perhaps inevitable that the killing of Osama bin Laden would serve as a rather dramatic blow to al-Qaeda popular morale. However, bin Laden's passing has been particularly difficult to accept for jihadi supporters in light of the litany of other losses the group has endured over the past 3 years. The list of top-tier casualties suffered by al-Qaeda includes, among others: Senior military field commander Abu Laith al-Liby, al-Qaeda Shura Council member Abu al-Hasan al-Masri, senior al-Qaeda explosives expert Abu Khabab al-Masri, senior al-Qaeda operational leader and spokesman Abu Mansour as-Shami, and al-Qaeda Shura Council member and presumed No. 3 in command of the group Mustafa Abu al-Yazid (a.k.a. Shaykh Saeed). Al-Yazid's death alone provoked the release of at least two different audio-recorded messages from al-Qaeda, including a confession from Dr. Ayman al-Zawahiri that he was "deeply saddened at the loss."[13] The killing of bin Laden has only managed to create an even larger gaping hole in al-Qaeda's already unsteady central hierarchy. In the wake of initial news reports about bin Laden's passing, one jihadi chat forum user "Abu Zubaydah" posted a message offering his deepest respects "to the family of the martyr . . . and also Shaykh Ayman Zawahiri, who in a single year lost Shaykh Saeed and now his other companion on the path . . . By Allah, it is a year of sorrow."[14]

With bin Laden now gone, the question naturally turns to who will be selected to replace his now vacant position as the overall commander of al-Qaeda. Media speculation in recent days has ranged wildly—from fugitive Yemeni-American cleric Anwar al-Awlaki to a relatively obscure Pakistani jihadi militant named Mohammed Ilyas Kashmiri. Though the identity of al-Qaeda's new top leader still remains uncertain, the far most likely candidate is al-Qaeda's present Deputy Commander Dr. Ayman al-Zawahiri. Al-Zawahiri, who merged his own Egyptian Islamic Jihad faction with al-Qaeda in 1998, has long stood alongside Osama bin Laden as his closest advisor. The former Egyptian pediatrician has both played a key operational role in organizing and overseeing international terrorist attacks, and has also simultaneously spearheaded al-Qaeda media efforts—personally appearing in dozens of audio and video recordings released by al-Qaeda's official media wing (in fact, far more often than bin Laden himself). With bin Laden gone, Ayman al-Zawahiri is by far the most recognizable face from among al-Qaeda's remaining central leadership. He is one of a dwindling number of commanders who can claim to be one of the original founders and Shura Council members of al-Qaeda. His essential credibility as an early pioneer of the jihadi movement in Egypt and Afghanistan would be quite difficult to match by any potential challenger vying for control of al-Qaeda.

As far as supporters chatting on top-tier al-Qaeda web forums, there simply has been no serious discussion of any potential bin Laden successors other than Dr. Ayman al-Zawahiri. Al-Qaeda's on-line constituents are so taken with the idea that al-Zawahiri will be the next leader of al-Qaeda that they have taken to casually referring to the group as "Jund Ayman" ("The Soldiers of Ayman"). Forum users have also taken it upon themselves to vigorously contest snarky comments from al-Qaeda critics that "Shaykh Usama made a mistake by merging al-Qaeda with Shaykh Ayman."[15] User "Muheb Ruyat al-Rahman" dismissed these prevalent critiques as "poison" from those "pretending to be sympathizers": "Do you really think our Shaykh Usama couldn't distinguish the worthless from the valuable, or the beautiful from the ugly? Do you think . . . that he was somehow tricked by Shaykh Ayman? Do you really believe that [bin Laden] . . . who refused to surrender his faith in jihad would simply give up on what he judged to be truthful and correct merely in order to satisfy Shaykh Ayman?"[16] Al-Rahman insisted, "Our Shaykh Usama, may Allah have mercy on him, is our Shaykh Ayman, and our Shaykh Ayman is our Shaykh Usama."[17]

Nevertheless, this is not to say that the ascension of Dr. Ayman al-Zawahiri to the top of al-Qaeda's hierarchy is by any means guaranteed, nor is it necessarily a fortunate development for the organization. Since beginning his career as a jihadi activist in Egypt, al-Zawahiri has acquired a notorious reputation as arrogant, self-serving, and unconscionably ruthless. As early as 1990, at al-Qaeda's own guesthouses in the Pakistani city of Peshawar, mujahideen fighters began to loudly grumble that too many Egyptians—primarily al-Zawahiri's cronies—were being appointed to senior positions in al-Qaeda. Accusations of preferential treatment and corruption

[13] http://www.al-faloja.info/vb/showthread.php?t=127650. July 30, 2010.
[14] http://as-ansar.com/vb/showthread.php?t=37762. May 2, 2011.
[15] http://shamikh1.net/vb/showthread.php?t=110085. May 16, 2011.
[16] http://shamikh1.net/vb/showthread.php?t=110085. May 16, 2011.
[17] http://shamikh1.net/vb/showthread.php?t=110085. May 16, 2011.

34

began to fly back and forth. Former al-Qaeda lieutenant Jamal al-Fadl later recalled during testimony in U.S. Federal court when he finally confronted Osama bin Laden to complain that "the camp was being run by Egyptian people and the guesthouse—the emir from the guesthouse—is Egyptian and everything [is] Egyptian people and [everyone is] from [the Egyptian] jihad group, and we have people from Nigeria, from Tunisia, from Siberia, [so] why is Egyptian people got more chance than other people run everything?"[18] Some of the dissidents within al-Qaeda felt too "embarrassed" to say this to bin Laden's face, while others—such as a Libyan fighter named Abu Tamim—were much more vocal with their concerns: "He say, why everything run by Egyptian people?"[19]

During an interview in 2007 with the London-based newspaper Al-Hayat, Sayyid Imam al-Sharif (a.k.a. "Dr. Fadl")—once a "leading figure" in Dr. Ayman al-Zawahiri's Egyptian Islamic Jihad (EIJ) movement and a founding member of al-Qaeda's own governing Shura Council—personally accused al-Zawahiri of being a "liar", a "gangster", and a "bandit." According to al-Sharif, "Ayman is a charlatan who used secrecy as a pretext . . . I can't think of anyone in Islamic history who has committed such deceit, fraud, falsification, and betrayal of trust . . . no one before Ayman al-Zawahiri."[20] When I raised the subject of al-Zawahiri's status of authority within al-Qaeda in a discussion with former Arab-Afghan mujahid Abdullah Anas, he sighed for a moment and chuckled to himself. "Can you imagine a great religion represented by al-Zawahiri?" he asked me. "It's a catastrophe."

In light of al-Zawahiri's obvious shortcomings, and the likelihood that he will one day meet an end analogous to that of bin Laden, it behooves us to examine the other potential leadership candidates among the top tier of al-Qaeda's inner sanctum. Those candidates include:

Abu Yahya al-Liby (a.k.a. Hassan Qaid)

Though he has undoubtedly far slimmer credentials than Dr. Ayman al-Zawahiri, Shaykh Abu Yahya al-Liby has nonetheless also become a strikingly influential figure in the international jihadist movement ever since his stunning escape in July 2005 from a high-security U.S. prison at Bagram air base (near Kabul). At the time of his initial capture in Karachi, Pakistan in the wake of the events of 9/11, Abu Yahya was at most a mid-ranking lieutenant within a faction of the Libyan Islamic Fighting Group (LIFG) directly allied with al-Qaeda. At the time, he was best known as an expert in computer media and Islamic jurisprudence. According to fellow former LIFG commander Noman Benotman, Abu Yahya "was a member of the Shariah committee of the LIFG, and he was known within the framework of the LIFG, and joined it relatively early on . . . almost in 1991 . . . He was there at the end of the Afghan Jihad, meaning with the LIFG . . . But he wasn't from amongst the top leadership."[21]

However, the combination of Abu Yahya's public speaking abilities, his natural charisma, and the compelling personal credential of having brazenly slipped out of America's highest-security prison in Afghanistan proved to be a powerful cocktail. Less than 6 months after fleeing Bagram, Abu Yahya began to appear in video recordings produced by al-Qaeda's official "As-Sahab Media Foundation"—so often, in fact, that his face has become virtually synonymous with As-Sahab. Over the last 5 years, Abu Yahya has been the principle featured spokesman for al-Qaeda in dozens of audio and video recordings released by As-Sahab—appearing more often than either Osama bin Laden or Ayman al-Zawahiri. Abu Yahya's recorded sermons are highly influential, and are recycled and often re-published by other likeminded terrorist organizations like Shabaab al-Mujahideen in Somalia. Though Abu Yahya has never been granted an official title in al-Qaeda's leadership to match that of bin Laden, al-Zawahiri, or Mustafa Abu al-Yazid, he is widely considered to be within the very top echelons of the organization—possibly even the new "No. 3" in the wake of al-Yazid's demise last year. Yet, as far as his former comrade Noman Benotman is concerned, Abu Yahya "was never, and I doubt will ever be, a military commander."[22]

Shaykh Atiyallah al-Liby (a.k.a. Atiyah Abd al-Rahman)

Shaykh Atiyallah al-Liby is another Libyan national within the top ranks of al-Qaeda who hails from the now-besieged coastal town of Misrata. According to the

[18] *United States* v. *Usama bin Laden, et al.* S(7) 98 Cr. 1023 (LBS). United States District Court, Southern District of New York. Trial Transcript, February 6, 2001. Page 322.
[19] *United States* v. *Usama bin Laden,* et al. S(7) 98 Cr. 1023 (LBS). United States District Court, Southern District of New York. Trial Transcript, February 6, 2001. Page 322.
[20] "Interview with Sayyid Imam al-Sharif." *Al-Hayat.* December 8–10, 2007.
[21] "Industry of Death: Abu Yahya al-Liby." *Al-Arabiya.* July 4, 2009.
[22] "Industry of Death: Abu Yahya al-Liby." Al-Arabiya. July 4, 2009.

U.S. State Department, Atiyallah first joined bin Laden in Afghanistan "as a teen-ager in the 1980s. Since then, he has gained considerable stature in al-Qa'ida as an explosives expert and Islamic scholar."[23] While in Afghanistan during the late 1990s, the Libyan also forged a relationship with a young Abu Musab al-Zarqawi in the western Afghan city of Herat.[24] He also joined bin Laden and his coterie of top aides as they fled under fire to the mountainous redoubt of Tora Bora late in the fall of 2001.[25]

Following the battle of Tora Bora, Shaykh Atiyallah publicly emerged as a key ideologue and spokesman on behalf of al-Qaeda's senior leadership. As part of that role, according to the U.S. Government, Atiyallah "recruits and facilitates talks with other Islamic groups to operate under al-Qaida" and "has been in regular contact with senior ranking al-Qaida leaders."[26] In fact, the Libyan al-Qaeda leader has been a major proponent of decentralizing al-Qaeda's network into an autonomous web of franchise affiliates. According to an essay written Atiyallah in 2004, the advantage of such a strategy is that "collective organized work is not affected by the loss of individuals, because individuals are easily replaced with others. The organization exists not on any individual; rather it operates as number of distributed responsibilities where the loss of individuals is redundant. This is one of the secrets of the effectiveness of al-Qaeda and their success in group operations."[27]

Since the death of Mustafa Abu al-Yazid, Shaykh Atiyallah has been making an increasingly frequent number of cameos in al-Qaeda audio and video recordings released by the As-Sahab Media Foundation. In his last appearance in a video released on March 18, 2011, he urged Libyan rebels to adopt an Islamist methodology and "avoid allying with the enemies of Allah."[28] He also sternly warned "the enemies of Allah, whether America or others, to even think about acts of aggression or interference in the country [of Libya]. Otherwise, the Army of Allah and the chivalrous men of Islam will make them forget the tragedies they faced previously."[29]

Abu Zaid al-Kuwaiti (a.k.a. Khaled al-Hussainan)

Though Shaykh Khaled al-Hussainan is a relatively new arrival to the jihad in Afghanistan, he is far older than most of al-Qaeda's new up-and-coming generation of leaders. Likewise, while he has had no major military experiences to speak of, al-Hussainan has other credentials that offer him a leg up within al-Qaeda's hierarchy—namely, that he was once a respected cleric at the Al-Albani mosque in Kuwait and a former state-sponsored lecturer at the Kuwaiti Ministry of Religious Endowments.[30] Al-Hussainan also reportedly worked as a preacher at the Saad al-Abdullah Academy, which is responsible for training Kuwaiti military officers. By 1996, Khaled al-Hussainan encountered his first brush with the law when he faced criminal charges in Kuwait in connection with what became known the "Desert Flogging" Case. Though he was later found innocent, al-Hussainan had been accused of joining with a group of radical Islamists in forcibly abducting two women and assaulting them with a whip in a remote location as punishment for "what they considered to be a shameful act."[31] In 2007, without any warning, al-Hussainan suddenly disappeared from his pulpit in Kuwait and traveled to Afghanistan, reportedly by crossing through Iranian territory. Less than 2 years later, in August 2009, al-Hussainan was first publicly identified by al-Qaeda's media wing as a prominent leader and spokesman for the group.[32]

That al-Hussainan is one of al-Qaeda's few remaining top-tier originally from the Arabian Peninsula (and a graduate of the Imam Muhammad bin Saud University in the Kingdom of Saudi Arabia) is hugely significant.[33] First of all, al-Qaeda's traditional wealthy financial donors based in the Gulf region are generally predisposed towards channeling their generous assistance to mujahideen organizations with prominent Saudi or Kuwaiti leaders with whom they feel most comfortable. Second, in countries like Afghanistan and Pakistan, the fact that al-Hussainan can say that he is from the same sacred soil as the holy city of Mecca and the Prophet Mohammed plays uniquely well among local Islamists. In video messages released by al-

[23] *http://www.rewardsforjustice.net/english/index.cfm?page=atiyah_abd.*
[24] *http://www.rewardsforjustice.net/english/index.cfm?page=atiyah_abd.*
[25] *http://www.rewardsforjustice.net/english/index.cfm?page=atiyah_abd.*
[26] *http://www.rewardsforjustice.net/english/index.cfm?page=atiyah_abd.*
[27] Atiyatullah, Louis. "The Badr Al-Riyadh Tape: A Well Organized al-Qaeda's Media Strategy Revealed." The Global Islamic Media Front (GIMF). 2004. Page 2.
[28] *http://shamikh1.net/vb/showthread.php?t=99893.* March 18, 2011.
[29] *http://shamikh1.net/vb/showthread.php?t=99893.* March 18, 2011.
[30] *http://www.islamhouse.com/ip/288149.* May 2011.
[31] "Industry of Death: Who is Khalid al-Hussainan?" *Al-Arabiya.* October 30, 2010.
[32] *http://www.al-faloja.info/vb/showthread.php?t=77715.* August 7, 2009.
[33] *http://www.islamhouse.com/ip/288149.*

Qaeda, al-Hussainan has boasted of "traveling in Afghanistan from village to village and from city to city and from province to province, and praise Allah, I speak in the mosques and encourage the Afghan people to perform Jihad and encourage them to stand by the Mujahideen and encourage them to expel the Crusaders who have corrupted the people and land."[34]

Though his background is exclusively clerical, Khaled al-Hussainan has claimed to be participating in actual armed combat with Afghan and coalition military forces. In August 2009, he issued an open message to U.S. President Barack Obama, boasting, "your soldiers besieged me. I was besieged by your soldiers for 10 hours. I was besieged by 30 tanks accompanied by helicopters and warplanes."[35] According to al-Hussainan, "We came to Afghanistan to be killed as martyrs in Allah's path. We came to Afghanistan for the hereafter. This is the fact which I want you to understand, Obama . . . We came to Afghanistan for Islam to dominate, not be dominated."[36]

Saif al-Adel (a.k.a. Mohammed al-Makkawi)

Saif al-Adel (sometimes also known as "Mohammed al-Makkawi") is a former Egyptian military officer who went on to become a top leader of the Egyptian Islamic Jihad, and a founding member of al-Qaeda's Shura Council. From early on, al-Adel served a critical role as al-Qaeda's security chief, and as a manager of its covert overseas operations. According to former al-Qaeda lieutenant Jamal al-Fadl, al-Adel earned a reputation as "one of the members very good with explosives . . . He trained people for explosives."[37] By the late 1990s, al-Adel's nefarious activities were well-known to U.S. law enforcement and he was indicted along with Osama bin Laden in the Southern District of New York (SDNY) for his role in the August 1998 bombings of two U.S. embassies in East Africa.[38] According to the mastermind of the September 11, 2001 terrorist attacks on the United States, Khalid Shaykh Mohammed, Saif al-Adel was also "involved in the 9/11 attack" and "knew the identity of the pilots who had been chosen when the Hamburg cell was picked in early 2000."[39]

Like other senior al-Qaeda leaders, in late 2001, al-Adel gathered his family and fled with bin Laden to their rallying point in the Tora Bora mountains. In a later treatise published by al-Qaeda, al-Adel recalled how the group had dwindled to "at best" 1,900 men, with at least 350 "heroes" lying dead on the battlefield. Facing potential annihilation, al-Qaeda divided their ranks: "some of them returned to their countries, whereas the rest stayed to take revenge from Americans and their allies."[40] Despite the capture of his wife and children in Tora Bora, Saif al-Adel managed to escape and continue in his role overseeing operations targeting coalition forces in southern Afghanistan. After a battle with U.S. forces in Kandahar in 2002, al-Adel insisted that "the Americans are not up to ground battles . . . They will not consider another experience in Kandahar, especially that the military force based in Kandahar has, by the grace of Allah, a level of the expertise that will make the U.S. a running joke for centuries to come."[41]

Facing a renewed hunt by the U.S. military, Saif al-Adel allegedly fled once again—this time to neighboring Iran, where he was reportedly detailed and placed under house arrest. Al-Adel's exact status in Iran has always been somewhat murky. Though some reports paint him as under the strict custody of Iranian intelligence agents, other information suggests that al-Adel may have continued playing an operational role in al-Qaeda from the open sanctuary of Iran. In May 2003, U.S. National security officials accused al-Adel of "giving the go-ahead" for a dramatic wave of suicide bombing attacks in Riyadh, Saudi Arabia that killed at least 34 people. According to one "senior administration" source quoted by the *Washington Post,* "there are some senior members of al Qaeda in Iran . . . who might have had a hand in this."[42]

---

[34] *http://www.al-faloja.info/vb/showthread.php?t=82666.* September 7, 2009.
[35] *http://www.al-faloja.info/vb/showthread.php?t=82666.* September 7, 2009.
[36] *http://www.al-faloja.info/vb/showthread.php?t=82666.* September 7, 2009.
[37] *United States* v. *Osama bin Laden,* et al. S(7) 98 Cr. 1023 (LBS). United States District Court, Southern District of New York. Trial Transcript, February 6, 2001. Page 244.
[38] *http://news.findlaw.com/cnn/docs/binladen/usbinladen-1a.pdf.*
[39] "Substitution for the Testimony of Khalid Sheikh Mohammed." *United States* v. *Zacarias Moussaoui.* Eastern District of Virginia (EDVA). Cr. No. 01–455–A. Defense Exhibit 941.
[40] *http://www.bkufus.com/images/img/indexe.php?subject=2&rec=14&tit=tit&pa=0.* January 2003.
[41] *http://www.bkufus.com/images/img/indexe.php?subject=2&rec=15&tit=tit&pa=0.* January 2003.
[42] Priest, Dana and Susan Schmidt. "Al Qaeda Figure Tied To Riyadh Bombings; U.S. Officials Say Leader Is In Iran With Other Terrorists." *Washington Post.* May 18, 2003. Page A24.

The controversial idea that a senior Sunni Muslim extremist like Saif al-Adel would choose to hide out in a fundamentalist Shiite state like Iran has not escaped the attention of al-Qaeda's sectarian followers. In 2008, when Dr. Ayman al-Zawahiri agreed to participate in an open Q&A session with al-Qaeda's supporters on the web, he was peppered with inquiries about Saif al-Adel. One questioner explained, "I want to be rid of this doubt: why is Shaykh Saif al-Adel present in Iran, which murders our sons, keeps our women prisoner, and has perverted our religion and Quran—and yet he suffers no harm from them? . . . His presence causes many question and exclamation marks. I ask you by Allah to clarify to us, O' our noble Shaykh."[43] Though al-Zawahiri acknowledged receiving these numerous questions about al-Adel, he refused to give any further explanation. "As for his question about the location of Saif al-Adel," al-Zawahiri replied dryly, "it is something I am unable to tell him."[44]

Despite recent reports indicating that al-Adel has finally left Iran and has returned to the Pakistani-Afghan border region, there are compelling reasons to believe that he will not be appointed as bin Laden's replacement in charge of al-Qaeda. Al-Adel has never served a public role in al-Qaeda, and has deliberately avoided taking any sort of political role within the organization or even being shown on camera. In fact, al-Adel has based his entire career in al-Qaeda in serving critical but low-key roles within the upper echelon of bin Laden's operational arm. Assuming that al-Adel has indeed rejoined al-Qaeda's central leadership in AFPAK, the question remains if someone with as many lingering question marks as Saif al-Adel could possibly jump the hierarchy of al-Qaeda and supersede others figures like Ayman al-Zawahiri or Abu Yahya al-Liby who already have much more established profiles among al-Qaeda's contemporary base.

Azzam al-Amriki (a.k.a. Adam Gadahn)

Adam Yehiye Gadahn is a convert to Islam originally from northern California. Raised on an isolated goat farm, Gadahn eventually moved south to Los Angeles to live with his grandmother. While in Los Angeles, Gadahn came into contact with a cell of computer-savvy al-Qaeda militants planning to aid Osama bin Laden in Afghanistan. In 1998, Gadahn moved to Pakistan and married an Afghani refugee. Shortly thereafter, Gadahn was allegedly recruited by 9/11 mastermind Khalid Shaykh Mohammed to assist in al-Qaeda's on-going media efforts.[45] In 2001, Gadahn made his first public appearance on behalf of al-Qaeda, when he lent his voice to help narrate an English-subtitled version of al-Qaeda's first official propaganda video, "The Destruction of the U.S.S. Cole."[46]

Since 2004, Adam Gadahn has appeared in dozens of video-recorded messages released by al-Qaeda. In 2005, in a video marking the fourth anniversary of 9/11, Gadahn explained in English the role of As-Sahab's multimedia in recruiting new al-Qaeda members:

"Allah is our witness that the numerous audio and videotapes issued by Shaykh Usama Bin Laden, Dr. Ayman al-Zawahiri, and other leaders of the jihad have not been released merely to dispel rumors of their death—or, as the Americans once ridiculously claimed, to send coded messages to their followers. No, these communiqués have been released to explain and propound the nature and goals of the worldwide jihad against America and the crusaders, and to convey our legitimate demands to friend and foe alike, so that the former may join us on this honorable and blessed path . . . ".[47]

Fingering an automatic weapon, Gadahn also added the following comments, swearing revenge on his own former hometown: "Yesterday, London and Madrid. Tomorrow, Los Angeles and Melbourne [Australia], God-willing . . . We love peace, but when the enemy violates that peace or prevents us from achieving it, then we love nothing better than the heat of battle, the echo of explosions, and [slitting] the throats of the infidels. When it comes to defending our religion, our freedom, and

---

[43] *http://myhesbah.com/v/showthread?t=174676*. April 2, 2008.
[44] *http://myhesbah.com/v/showthread?t=174676*. April 2, 2008.
[45] *http://www.defenselink.mil/news/transcript_ISN10024.pdf*. Page 17.
[46] As-Sahab Media Foundation. "The State of the Ummah" (a.k.a. "The Destruction of the U.S.S. Cole"). Released: 2001.
[47] As-Sahab Media Foundation. "A Message to the People of the West from the fighting brother Azzam the American on the Fourth Anniversary of the Battles of New York and Washington." *http://www.as-sahaab.com*. MPEG Video; 12 minutes in length. November 6, 2005.

our brothers in faith, every one of us is Mohammed Atta. Every one of us is Jamal Lindsey, and every one of us is Mohammed Boieri."[48]

Of all the individuals discussed herein, Adam Gadahn likely has the slimmest chance of ever ascending the ranks much farther beyond his current position as a spokesman and media advisor. He has no formal clerical or military credentials to speak of, and while his proficiency in speaking Arabic is improving, it is still quite poor. Like Ayman al-Zawahiri, Gadahn appears to be obsessed with his own celebrity, spewing an endless train of childish threats for the benefit of television cameras. Even with his conversion to Islam and the dramatic destruction of his own U.S. passport, the fact that Gadahn is a Caucasian American with Jewish (and even Zionist) roots would be difficult for many Islamists to swallow. Gadahn may serve at times as a useful propaganda tool for al-Qaeda to harass the White House and the American public, but he hardly stands out as the most capable figure to actually lead a terrorist organization based in South Asia.

(IV) THE QUESTION OF AL-QAEDA'S REGIONAL AFFILIATES

Prior to 9/11, Osama bin Laden's principle obsession was on building a single armed force on a "Solid Foundation" with a centralized leadership under his control. According to founding al-Qaeda Shura Council member Mamdouh Mahmud Salim (a.k.a. Abu Hajer al-Iraqi), "Abu Abdullah [bin Laden] had tendency to favor a policy of centralization . . . and felt obligated to assemble the Arabs in one location, train and prepare them to be a single mobilized fighting brigade."[49] However, bin Laden had apparently overestimated the importance of group centralization, neglecting the substantial benefits afforded by al-Qaeda's loose, amalgamated infrastructure. Already by the late 1980s, those around bin Laden warned him that their attempts to create strict administration and hierarchy within al-Qaeda were ending in disaster. Mamdouh Salim—appointed by bin Laden to assist him in the regimentation of the Arabs in Afghanistan—admitted in mujahideen memoirs, "we tried our best to correct the brothers, but I should admit that . . . I was mistaken about the task of management. I thought of people what I had read about them in books—if you were to say to someone, 'Fear Allah', then that's fine, he would fear Allah! . . . I believed that just like I could flip a switch to make a light turn on and off, I could also similarly handle people!"[50]

For al-Qaeda, the real turning point came in December 2001, when groups of hardened al-Qaeda fighters attempted to make a dramatic last stand against U.S.-backed Afghan militiamen at a cave complex in the Tora Bora mountains, near the Pakistani border. The cream of al-Qaeda's leadership, including bin Laden himself, had gathered in Tora Bora for what seemed like a fool's errand: To fight a mismatched conventional military battle against an adversary with total air dominance and far more sophisticated battlefield weapons. U.S. tactical airstrikes smothered hundreds of fighters to dust: "there was no difference between the night and the day: the sky was raining fire and the Earth was erupting volcanoes."[51] Abortive attempts at regrouping and retreating caused the deaths of possibly hundreds of fleeing al-Qaeda fighters caught underneath a hail of cluster bombs. As a result of the defeats at Tora Bora and 3 months later at Shah-i-Kot, "almost all remaining al-Qaeda forces" fled across the border with Pakistan seeking refuge in the remote, mountainous, and "lightly governed" frontier provinces.[52]

Faced with a resounding defeat on the peaks of Tora Bora, a group of high-ranking al-Qaeda commanders decided to fundamentally re-think Osama bin Laden's military campaign against the West and to embrace the development of a more diffuse and self-sufficient network of international operatives. In 2002 and 2003, al-Qaeda's shift in strategy became noticeable following a series of dramatic kamikaze bombing attacks targeting Westerners in a host of countries, from Indonesia to Morocco. Al-Qaeda's then-official website—the Al-Neda Center for Islamic Studies and Research—acknowledged that these attacks marked a new phase in evolution: "the al-Qaeda Organization has adopted a strategy in its war with the Americans based on expanding the battlefield and exhausting the enemy, who spread his interests

[48] As-Sahab Media Foundation. "A Message to the People of the West from the fighting brother Azzam the American on the Fourth Anniversary of the Battles of New York and Washington." http://www.as-sahaab.com. MPEG Video; 12 minutes in length. November 6, 2005.
[49] Muhammad, Basil. Al-Ansaru l'Arab fi Afghanistan. The Committee for Islamic Benevolence Publications; ©1991. Page 199.
[50] Muhammad, Basil. Al-Ansaru l'Arab fi Afghanistan. The Committee for Islamic Benevolence Publications; ©1991. Page 196.
[51] Azzam, Abdullah. The Lofty Mountain. Azzam Publications. London; UK. ©2003. Page 136.
[52] The 9/11 Commission Report. Final Report of the National Commission on Terrorist Attacks Upon the United States. July 22, 2004. Page 338.

39

over the globe, with successive and varied blows . . . Expanding the battlefield has invaluable benefits. The enemy, who needed to protect his country only, realized that he needed to protect his huge interests in every country. The more diversified and distant the areas in which operations take place, the more exhausting it becomes for the enemy, the more he needs to stretch his resources, and the more he becomes terrified."[53] By mid-2004, nascent al-Qaeda franchise organizations were already well ensconced inside both Saudi Arabia and Iraq. Today, similar al-Qaeda franchises have expanded their reach even further into Indonesia, Yemen, Algeria, Somalia, Lebanon, and the Palestinian territories. These upstart regional branches are capable of operating independently of al-Qaeda's central leadership in Afghanistan—and though the immediate purpose of forming these branches was to ramp up local activity in particular countries of interest—the growing affiliate factions often have expansive ambitions just as grandiose as those of Osama bin Laden himself.

Al-Qaeda's decision to branch out and form semi-autonomous regional affiliates has not been without its drawbacks. In Iraq, even as al-Qaeda's local leader Abu Musab al-Zarqawi drew international media attention (rivaling that paid to bin Laden) for his unrelenting campaign of suicide bombings and beheadings, al-Zarqawi's stubborn insistence on doing things in his own particular style caused countless problems for al-Qaeda and other Sunni insurgent groups. According to fellow insurgents (including some acknowledged former Zarqawi allies), al-Qaeda fighters are responsible for adopting arrogant, totalitarian measures in Iraq that have acutely undermined their popular image in the Islamic community as "chivalrous knights" working to safeguard justice and the innocent. In October 2007, one such estranged insurgent partner, the "Iraqi Jihad Union" (IJU), issued an open call to al-Qaeda's leaders: "What is happening out in the field is indeed a disaster and we hope that you have merely been misinformed about [these events]. However, it will be an even greater disaster if you are, in fact, well-informed about these matters."[54] The IJU fingered al-Qaeda fighters as the guilty culprits behind the slaughter and mutilation of their own Sunni Muslim comrades: "To make things worse, they dug up their bodies from the graves, further mutilated them, beheaded them, and showed them off from their vehicles while driving through the towns. They even killed our men's wives and children."[55] Yet another armed faction—"Hamas al-Iraq"—scoffed in a separate statement to its supporters, "the al-Qaeda network has actually made people here think that the occupation forces are merciful and humane by comparison."[56]

Only 2 years after bragging that al-Qaeda had "broken the back" of America with a barrage of suicide bombings in Iraq, Dr. Ayman al-Zawahiri was forced to reappear in April 2008 in order to defend Zarqawi's cruel methodology in the face of sharp criticism from fellow Muslims. During a public Arabic-language Q&A session sponsored by al-Qaeda, one anonymous participant (who scornfully introduced himself as "Your Geography Teacher") jeered at al-Zawahiri, "Do you consider the killing of women and children to be Jihad? I challenge you and your organization to do that in Tel Aviv . . . Or is it easier to kill Muslims in the markets? Maybe it is necessary [for you] to take some geography lessons, because your maps only show the Muslims' states."[57] With a touch of anger building in his voice, Dr. al-Zawahiri insisted, "We haven't killed the innocents, not in Baghdad, nor in Morocco, nor in Algeria, nor anywhere else." After a moment of reflection, he added, "And if there is any innocent who was killed in the Mujahideen's operations, then it was either an unintentional error, or out of necessity as in cases of . . . the taking of human shields by the enemy."[58]

Nor have things gone especially well for al-Qaeda in the Kingdom of Saudi Arabia, where the group's local leadership was forced to flee the country or else be wiped out in a dragnet by security forces. During a 2006 interview in London, the prominent Saudi Islamist dissident Dr. Saad al-Faqih suggested that the problem stemmed from a critical shortage of locally-based skilled commanders following the death of the founder of the Saudi al-Qaeda branch, Yusuf al-Ayyiri: "Al-Ayyiri . . . was appointed by Bin Laden . . . probably before [9/11]. He is capable, you know. You know that this man is capable, right? [Al-Ayyiri] is a learned scholar,

---

[53] Al-Neda Center for Islamic Studies and Research. "The Operation of 11 Rabi al-Awwal: The East Riyadh Operation and Our War With the United States and its Agents." *http://www.faroq.org/news/news.php?id.* August 2003.
[54] *http://www.alboraq.info/showthread?t=33995.* October 5, 2007.
[55] *http://www.alboraq.info/showthread?t=33995.* October 5, 2007.
[56] *http://www.alboraq.info/showthread?t=33728.* October 2, 2007.
[57] *http://myhesbah.com/v/showthread?t=174676.* April 2, 2008.
[58] *http://myhesbah.com/v/showthread?t=174676.* April 2, 2008.

highly professional as a fighter, he is powerful in his articulation, has a dominating personality, he is a strategist. He knows what he is doing."[59] However, in the absence of al-Ayyiri, al-Qaeda's strategy in Saudi Arabia turned "hopeless": "Their strategy in Saudi Arabia is in shambles . . . I see it as, in their own standards, very stupid strategy . . . Bin Laden was not fortunate to have an intelligent, capable person after al-Ayyiri. All the persons who came after al-Ayyiri were good military leaders but very bad strategists, very bad tacticians."[60]

In listing their various shortcomings, Dr. al-Faqih particularly noted the inexplicable failure of Saudi al-Qaeda leaders to conduct their activities in a way that might possibly have some popular appeal among ordinary Saudis. Al-Faqih scoffed, "when you confront them with the question, 'why do you go to foreigners and leave [Prince] Nayif?', they can't answer. They answer very stupid answers. Sloganistic answers . . . This is a very naive literal interpretation of the prophet's teaching."[61] As a result, not only has the "cadre from before the Iraqi war been hit very hard by the regime", but moreover, "people who had some sort of intention to join al-Qaeda inside the country changed their mind. They also lost in terms of sympathy and understanding."[62] According to Dr. al-Faqih, "al-Qaeda did not lose because of the technology of the Saudi government, did not lose because of the effective, the 'effective' media, cultural, and security campaign, it did not lose because of the support from the Americans and others. It lost because of its own mistakes."[63] After a heavy sigh, he confessed, "I cannot understand why they planned it this way."[64]

While al-Qaeda's regional efforts in Iraq and Saudi Arabia may have suffered debilitating setbacks in recent years, the picture could not be any more different in nearby Yemen—where a growing al-Qaeda branch (known simply as "al-Qaeda in the Arabian Peninsula") not only has threatened to undermine the stability of the central government in Sanaa, but moreover, has demonstrated its ability to launch repeated and sophisticated international terrorist attacks targeting the U.S. homeland. Without doubt, the defining event for al-Qaeda's network in Yemen came in 2008 with the unexpected arrival of numerous Saudi Arabian al-Qaeda operatives who had recently been freed after years of detention in Guantanamo Bay, Cuba. An influential partnership was formed between the remnants of al-Qaeda's Saudi branch and loyal Yemeni disciples of Osama bin Laden—including his former personal secretary, Abu Basir al-Wahishi, and a graduate of Bin Laden's notorious Al-Farouq training camp near Kandahar, Qassim al-Rimi. In total, at least 11 former Gitmo detainees from Saudi Arabia returned to al-Qaeda, most of them by fleeing political rehabilitation centers and crossing the Saudi border into Yemen.

Throughout 2009, a slew of latent warnings emerged indicating that AQAP was developing advanced bomb-making skills, including the ability to circumvent heightened security measures at airports and other sensitive installations. Over the space of several months, al-Qaeda's network in Yemen released successive video recordings showing the fabrication of elaborate explosive devices, including bombs carefully hidden in picture frames and video cassette boxes. Then, in August 2009, AQAP claimed responsibility for its most sophisticated operation yet: The attempted assassination of the Saudi Deputy Interior Minister by a "surrendering" al-Qaeda member with a bomb hidden in his underwear. In an official communiqué released days later by AQAP, the group trumpeted the "first-of-its-kind" suicide operation by the baby-faced Abdullah Asseri who "was able to enter the palace . . . get past his bodyguards, and ignited his explosive device . . . after he already managed to pass through all the security checkpoints at the airports in Najran and Jeddah."[65]

In a video testimonial produced by AQAP and first broadcast in September 2009, Asseri bragged about the impressive technical innovations of locally-based al-Qaeda bombmakers:

"This is my ammunition . . . Allah has made this available to the mujahideen . . . The idol-worshipping tyrants of the Saudi family thought that they closed the doors on the face of the mujahideen, by banning all explosive substances from the markets. But Allah made available to us something they cannot handle . . . Allah willing, we will come to you with only 50, 100 or 200 grams. Allah willing, our brothers in the explosives department will release some instruc-

---

[59] Author's interview with Dr. Saad al-Faqih at his residence in London; U.K. February 2006.
[60] Author's interview with Dr. Saad al-Faqih at his residence in London; U.K. February 2006.
[61] Author's interview with Dr. Saad al-Faqih at his residence in London; U.K. February 2006.
[62] Author's interview with Dr. Saad al-Faqih at his residence in London; U.K. February 2006.
[63] Author's interview with Dr. Saad al-Faqih at his residence in London; U.K. February 2006.
[64] Author's interview with Dr. Saad al-Faqih at his residence in London; U.K. February 2006.
[65] Al-Qaeda in the Arabian Peninsula (AQAP). "Statement Claiming Responsibility for the Assassination Attempt on the Tyrant Mohammed bin Nayif al-Saud." August 29, 2009.

41

tive videos about how you can blow up the enemies of Allah with simple ingredients available to all which they cannot ban, except if they kill everyone or close all the stores. Sometimes you will be amazed that explosives can be made with things we even eat."[66]

On Christmas day 2009, Nigerian national Umar Farouk Abdulmutallab—armed with a remarkably similar explosive device provided to him by AQAP and concealed in his underwear—attempted to bring down a civilian airliner packed with holiday travelers en route from Amsterdam to Detroit.

In the months since the failed airline bombing over Detroit, AQAP has expressed particular pride in the fact that their recruit Umar Abdulmutallab was so successful in evading strict international airline security procedures. During a propaganda video produced by al-Qaeda's network in Yemen, an unseen narrator smugly insists, "security and military solutions won't help providing security for the Americans and their allies, as after 8 years of big and continuous spending for the cause of advancing the security abilities, the mujahideen were able, with the grace of Allah, to infiltrate all the boundaries; the brother Umar Farouk—may Allah release him—took off and passed through five international airports, including the Dutch airport in Amsterdam, and neither their technology nor machines were able to uncover the manufactured device."[67] The leadership of al-Qaeda even published an eye-catching article on this subject in the official AQAP on-line magazine, titled, "Secrets of the Manufactured Device":

"Among the secrets of the device is that it included the study of the [currently] used scanning machines inside airports and other places, whether the security side or the technical side in America and Europe . . . studying all these gaps took place, and with the grace of Allah what we wished for has occurred; the intended martyr brother crossed four continents—Asia, then African, then Europe, then America—and he passed through four international airports that have strict procedures . . . The mujahideen have [also] acquired a highly-explosive material with power that exceeds the classic high explosives like 'PETN' and 'TNT' and 'RDX' and others, and it is being prepared and tested."[68]

Until quite recently, the notion of such complex planning for transnational terrorist activities taking place outside the narrow confines of Osama bin Laden's inner circle in Afghanistan would have seemed baffling and radically controversial to most observers.

The re-organized al-Qaeda network based in Yemen has also benefited from the contributions of Yemeni-American cleric Shaykh Anwar al-Awlaki, a charismatic, English-speaking missionary who had evolved from a mainstream "moderate" voice into one of the most passionate global advocates for violent jihad in any language. On his internet blog—popular among British, Canadian, and American Muslims—al-Awlaki openly applauded al-Qaeda attacks on Yemeni security forces: "May this be the beginning of the greatest jihad, the jihad of the Arabian Peninsula that would free the heart of the Islamic world from the tyrants who are deceiving the Ummah and standing between us and victory."[69] Al-Awlaki has been publicly fingered by U.S. officials as the responsible party in turning Umar Abdulmutallab towards al-Qaeda. Speaking in a video interview produced by AQAP, al-Awlaki enthused that the Christmas day airline bomb plot had "accomplished goals for the mujahideen and it is considered a reply and terrorizing operation to the Americans, and this operation showed the gaps in the American security instruments whether it be intelligence-wise or in the security. In the American airports they spend more than 40 million dollars and yet the Mujahid Umar Farouk was able to pass these security instruments. And also the intelligence admits that it had put him under surveillance and in spite of that he was able to reach the heart of America to Detroit. So the operation accomplished great successes though it did not kill even one person, in spite of that it accomplished great successes." After a pause, al-Awlaki added, "About the brother Umar Farouk, he is also from my students, and also I

[66] Al-Malahem Media Wing; al-Qaeda in the Arabian Peninsula (AQAP). "The Progeny of Mohammed bin Maslamah." Released on August 29, 2009.
[67] Al-Malahem Media Wing; al-Qaeda in the Arabian Peninsula (AQAP). "America and the Final Trap." Released on May 26, 2010.
[68] Al-Malahem Media Wing; al-Qaeda in the Arabian Peninsula (AQAP). "Secrets of the Manufactured Device." Sada al-Malahem Magazine. Issue No. 12; Released on February 14, 2010.
[69] Al-Awlaki, Anwar. "The Army of Yemen Confronts the Mujahideen." August 1, 2009. Posted on: http://www.anwar-alawlaki.com.

am very proud that the likes of Umar Farouk are from my students and I support what he did."[70]

Perhaps the most disturbing aspect of AQAP's interest in launching international terrorist attacks on the United States is their long-running obsession with conceiving plots aimed at causing "catastrophic" damage to the American economy. In October 2002, following a suicide bomb attack on a French supertanker off the coast of Yemen, al-Qaeda's Politburo lost no time in formally praising the operation for "revealing the true danger the mujahideen pose to the strategic, commercial, and military interests of the enemy":

"If a boat that once cost us less than $1,000 managed to ruin a destroyer worth over $1 billion (its symbolic value beyond measure), and a similar boat managed to devastate an oil tanker of such great magnitude, imagine the extent of the danger that threatens the West's commercial lifeline which is petrol. This region sits on the largest [oil] reserves, owns the largest quantities and contains [the industry's] most important passages and lanes. The operation that struck the French oil tanker is not merely an attack against a tanker—it is an attack against international oil transport lines and all its various connotations."[71]

When it was still based in Saudi Arabia, AQAP published a treatise titled, "Bin Laden and the Oil Weapon", in which the affiliate group argued that because "the United States will remain dependent on the Middle East in the near future, its oil will continue to be an easy target for all the enemies of the United States . . . It is imperative that we strike petroleum interests in all regions that the United States benefits from, and not only in the Middle East. The goal is to cut off its imports or reduce them by all means. The targeting of oil interests includes oil production wells, export pipelines, loading platforms, tankers—and anything else that will deprive the United States of oil, force it to make decisions that it has avoided having to make for a long time, disrupt and stifle its economy, and threaten its economic and political future."[72]

In early 2008, after al-Qaeda moved its local operations from Saudi Arabia to Yemen, the reconstituted AQAP published an approving interview with a most wanted Saudi al-Qaeda suspect Nayef Bin Mohammed al-Qahtani (a.k.a. Abu Humam al-Qahtani). Again endorsing the concept of striking at petroleum resources, al-Qahtani reasoned, "if the enemy's interests in the Arabian Peninsula were stricken, and his supply of oil was cut off, and the oil refineries were out of order, this would cause the enemy to collapse—and he won't merely withdraw from Iraq and Afghanistan, but would face total collapse. If he were to be struck hard from various places, then he would scatter and turn around and flee forlornly from the land of the Muslims."[73]

Given the high-profile role that AQAP has played in masterminding not only the "Underwear" bomber Abdulmutallab, but also more recently, a plot to smuggle explosive devices into U.S.-bound aircraft via UPS cargo shipments, AQAP's passionate interest in launching "strategic" attacks aimed at devastating the U.S. economy can be ignored only at our own peril. It is also a telling reminder of how, thanks to the new affiliate network of global franchises, the underlying al-Qaeda terrorist threat to the U.S. homeland is, in some ways, unchanged by the death of Osama bin Laden.

(V) THE "HOMEGROWNS": AL-QAEDA AS AN IDEOLOGY

Even further beyond al-Qaeda's existence as an organization and then as a franchise model is al-Qaeda as a political ideology. Given his obsession with group centralization, for many years, bin Laden failed to fully grasp how the relative "openness" of his movement and the perceived lack of hierarchy appealed to young jihadist recruits. In the world of al-Qaeda and the Arab-Afghans, even the most junior of operatives could potentially gain high status within the movement by either demonstrating useful skills, or else by volunteering to sacrifice themselves on behalf

[70] Al-Malahem Media Wing; al-Qaeda in the Arabian Peninsula (AQAP). "A Premiere and Exclusive Interview with the Islamic Preacher Sheikh Anwar Al-Awlaki." Released on May 22, 2010.

[71] Al-Neda Center for Islamic Studies and Research. "Statement from the al-Qaeda Organization Regarding the Explosion Targeting the Christian Oil Tanker in Yemen." Al-neda.com. October 13, 2002.

[72] Al-Bassam, Adeeb. "Bin Laden and the Oil Weapon." Sawt al-Jihad ("Voice of Jihad") Magazine; Issue No. 30. Al-Qaeda's Committee in the Arabian Peninsula (Saudi Arabia). Published: February 8, 2007.

[73] "A Meeting With One of the Most Wanted." Al-Malahem Media Wing; al-Qaeda in the Arabian Peninsula (AQAP). Sada al-Malahem Magazine. Issue No. 1; January 12, 2008.

of the mission. In other words, al-Qaeda offered an equal opportunity at fame and recognition to nearly any sympathetic soul willing to risk death or imprisonment. When agents from the U.S. Federal Bureau of Investigation (FBI) apprehended a junior al-Qaeda operative who helped build the suicide truck bombs used to attack two U.S. embassies in East Africa in 1998, he boasted of his own role in the plot and explained that he "was attracted to Usama Bin Ladin and the group Al Qaeda because it did not matter what nationality you were" and because al-Qaeda members did not explicitly follow "orders from a chain of command" in the same way as more traditional terrorist organizations.[74]

In retrospect, it now appears that it was not bin Laden, but rather his younger and more web-savvy lieutenants who truly championed the idea of spreading al-Qaeda as an ideology, including among homegrown extremists living in non-Muslim countries. One of those lieutenants was the founder of al-Qaeda's franchise affiliate in Saudi Arabia, Yusuf al-Ayyiri. Addressing those who had criticized al-Qaeda for killing innocent Arab civilians during the May 2003 attacks in Riyadh, al-Ayyiri scoffed, "Whoever asks why in [Saudi Arabia] should ask himself—if he was honest—why in Chechnya, why in Kabul, why in Jerusalem, why in Bali, and why in Mombassa. These countries are ruled by agent Karzai-type rulers and occupied by Americans or Jews who are considered infidels and untrustworthy in Allah's book." Moreover, according to al-Ayyiri, "this war is based on a strategy to widen the battlefield. The entire world has become a battlefield in practice and not in theory."[75]

Al-Ayyiri's strategy for developing a global "homegrown" terrorist movement has had an astonishing impact in motivating new faces to try and join al-Qaeda's cause—if not directly, then indirectly. Among both Arabic and English-speaking al-Qaeda supporters, one of al-Ayyiri's books has been particularly popular and enduring: "Constants on the Path of Jihad" ("Thawabit ala Darb al-Jihad"). The book attracted so much attention that fugitive AQAP cleric Shaykh Anwar al-Awlaki dedicated an entire lecture series to explaining al-Ayyiri's underlying message in "Constants on the Path of Jihad" to an English-speaking audience:

"Jihad does not end with the disappearance of a person. Jihad must continue regardless because it does not depend on any particular leader or individual . . . Jihad does not depend on any particular land. It is global. When the Muslim is in his land, he performs jihad . . . No borders or barriers stop it. The message cannot be conveyed without jihad. If a particular people or nation is classified as . . . 'the people of war' in the Shariah, that classification applies to them all over the earth. Islam cannot be customized to suit the conditions where you are, for instance Europe."[76]

According to Awlaki, al-Ayyiri also instructed that "victory" cannot be limited to mere "military victories" alone, and should also include "sacrifice. The Mujahid sacrificing 'his self' and his wealth is victory. Victory of your idea, your religion. If you die for your religion, your death will spread the da'wa . . . Allah chooses Shuhada (martyrs) from amongst the believers. This is a victory."[77]

By early 2003, jihadi recruiters in Europe who had previously encouraged others to travel to training camps in Afghanistan, Bosnia-Herzegovina, and Chechnya began radically changing their message. Just as with al-Ayyiri and al-Awlaki, their new philosophy emphasized the individual nature and responsibility of jihad. At a conference in Leicester organized by the radical Al-Muhajiroun faction in October 2002, Abu Hamza al-Masri (a.k.a. Mustafa Kamel) admonished his audience, "We need to resist, we need to fight, even alone. And you can't go now to learn in Afghanistan or Eritrea as before. Now, a war zone is a war zone. There is no need for camping, there is no facilities for camping . . . A lot of the skills you need for the frontline, you can learn from here . . . Where are you? What can you do in

[74] Government Exhibit GX–6 (Interview of Mohammed Sadiq Odeh by FBI Agent John Anticev). *U.S.* v. *Usama Bin Laden, et al.* S(7) 98 Cr. 1023 (LBS). United States District Court, Southern District of New York.

[75] Al-Neda Center for Islamic Studies and Research. "The Operation of 11 Rabi al-Awwal: The East Riyadh Operation and Our War With the United States and its Agents." *http://www.faroq.org/news/news.php?id.* August 2003.

[76] Shaykh Anwar Al Awlaki. "Constants on the Path of Jihad" ("Thawaabit Ala' Darb Al-Jihad.") Audio recording transcribed at *http://sabiluna.sitesled.com/Constants%20on%20The%20Path%20of%20Jihad.pdf.*

[77] Shaykh Anwar Al Awlaki. "Constants on the Path of Jihad" ("Thawaabit Ala' Darb Al-Jihad.") Audio recording transcribed at *http://sabiluna.sitesled.com/Constants%20on%20The%20Path%20of%20Jihad.pdf.*

44

your area?"[78] Al-Muhajiroun leader Shaykh Omar Bakri Mohammed echoed these comments and added, "the Ummah [should] know it is obligatory upon them to engage in . . . preparation and to engage in the jihad. And each one must find their own way. There is no need yourself to contact somebody here or there. You find your own way! Sincerely, you will get it. You do not want to put someone else in trouble. You, look for yourself! . . . Seek it! You will get it!"[79]

Surprisingly, rather than al-Qaeda's central leadership, it is arguably al-Qaeda's local affiliate in Yemen that has actually expended the greatest amount of entrepreneurial efforts in trying to mobilize homegrown jihadists and inciting them into action. Six months after the botched "Underwear" bomb plot involving Umar Abdulmutallab, AQAP released the first issue of a new English-language propaganda magazine titled "Inspire." An article from the first issue, "Make a Bomb in the Kitchen of Your Mom", explains:

"There are many Muslims who have the zeal to defend the ummah but their vision is unclear. They believe that in order to defend the ummah they need to travel and join the mujahideen elsewhere and they must train in their camps. But we tell the Muslims in America and Europe: There is a better choice and easier one to give support to your ummah. That is individual work inside the West such as the operations of [Fort Hood shooter] Nidal Hassan and [failed Times Square bomber] Faisal Shahzad . . . My Muslim brother, who wants to support the religion of Allah: do not make too many calculations and forecasting of the results and consequences. It is true that Umar Farouk and his brothers Nidal Hassan and Shahzad were imprisoned, but they have become heroes and icons that are examples to be followed . . . My Muslim brother: we are conveying to you our military training right into your kitchen to relieve you of the difficulty of traveling to us. If you are sincere in your intentions to serve the religion of Allah, then all what you have to do is enter your kitchen and make an explosive device that would damage the enemy."[80]

The second issue of AQAP's "Inspire" Magazine once again returned to the subject of individual jihad. Suggested tips included in the magazine urged would-be al-Qaeda recruits "coming from the West", "you might be asked by the mujahidin why you didn't partake in the jihad inside your country . . . Many will tell you that attacking the enemy in their backyard is one of the best ways to help the jihad . . . Put yourself in the shoes of the leadership for a moment. They have with them an individual who is not wanted by the intelligence services and they could use that person to further the Islamic cause. That person is you. I strongly recommend all the brothers and sisters coming from the West to consider attacking the West in its own backyard . . . These types of individual attacks are nearly impossible for them to contain."[81] The same magazine also featured plans for "the ultimate mowing machine", an "idea to use a pickup truck as a mowing machine, not to mow grass but mow down the enemies of Allah."[82] Above all, however, the magazine urged that "the best operation . . . is the one where you come up with an innovative idea that the authorities have not yet turned their attention to, and that leads to maximum casualties or—equally important—maximum economic losses."[83]

The identity of the reputed "genius" behind AQAP's latest propaganda coup is symbolic of the evolving terrorist threat posed by self-selecting "lone wolf" extremists. U.S. law enforcement and intelligence agencies believe that "Inspire" Magazine was created on behalf of AQAP by an American citizen and former resident of Charlotte, North Carolina, Samir Khan. In 2004, at the age of 18, Khan acquired a widespread reputation for his brash militancy on his well-traveled English-language blog, "InshallahShaheed" (Martyrdom God-willing). The blog routinely extolled the virtues of bin Laden and other al-Qaeda leaders, along with terrorist attacks in Iraq and elsewhere. Yet, for all his threats and internet tough talk, in real life, Khan looked far more the part of hapless computer nerd than deadly assassin. Nonetheless, in October 2009, 2 months before Umar Abdulmutallab boarded a flight headed

---

[78] Speech given at "Iraq Today Mecca Tomorrow." National Conference held in Leicester, United Kingdom; organized by Al-Muhajiroun, P.O. Box 349 London N9 7RR. October 27, 2002.
[79] Speech given at "Iraq Today Mecca Tomorrow." National Conference held in Leicester, United Kingdom; organized by Al-Muhajiroun, P.O. Box 349 London N9 7RR. October 27, 2002.
[80] "Make a Bomb in the Kitchen of Your Mom." *Inspire Magazine*. Al-Malahem Media Wing; al-Qaeda in the Arabian Peninsula (AQAP). Issue No. 1; Released on July 11, 2010.
[81] *Inspire Magazine*. Al-Malahem Media Wing; al-Qaeda in the Arabian Peninsula (AQAP). Issue No. 2; Released on October 11, 2010. Page 24.
[82] *Inspire Magazine*. Al-Malahem Media Wing; al-Qaeda in the Arabian Peninsula (AQAP). Issue No. 2; Released on October 11, 2010. Page 24.
[83] *Inspire Magazine*. Al-Malahem Media Wing; al-Qaeda in the Arabian Peninsula (AQAP). Issue No. 2; Released on October 11, 2010. Page 24.

45

to the United States, the aspiring suburban warrior Samir Khan left his own home in America and traveled to Yemen, where he promptly disappeared and presumably joined al-Qaeda.[84] In a letter published recently in "Inspire", Khan has since confessed his surprise at being allowed by U.S. Federal authorities to join AQAP unhindered: "I was quite open about my beliefs on-line and it didn't take a rocket scientist to figure out that I was al Qaeda to the core."[85]

Nor is Samir Khan alone. Internet chat forums run by al-Qaeda and likeminded jihadi movements have become beacons for a variety of extremists searching for a path to infamy in the guiding hands of al-Qaeda. In April 2010, when the Pakistani Taliban claimed responsibility for an attempted bomb plot in New York's Times Square, they chose to release their claim via an exclusive English-language al-Qaeda chat forum. One of the forum administrators—a mysterious "lone wolf" militant calling himself "Asadullah al-Shishani" ("the Lion of Allah from Chechnya")—immediately replied congratulating the Pakistani Taliban on their operation, and further offering to provide "help" in distributing their on-line propaganda.[86]

Two months later, user "Asadullah al-Shishani" posted his own homemade song on al-Qaeda's top-tier forums in honor of al-Qaeda's slain "No. 3" leader Mustafa Abu al-Yazid. The lyrics to the English-language song included the lines, "You are a real hero, O' Mustafa Abu Yazid. You spent your whole life fighting, Until you fell down Shaheed. You are a real terror, Against America. You sent their soldiers running, With shots of your Pee-Ka . . . Asadullah Alshishani salutes you. And he prays for the day, That he meets you in Jannah And is killed as a Fidaye. And I pray for the day, O that day, When I'm killed as a Fidaye."[87] This was quickly followed by the web release of yet another song performed in English by al-Shishani titled, "When the Jew's Blood Reds my Knife, then my Life is Free from Strife":

"Hiding behind rocks and trees, I'll find them with greatest ease. Make them get down on their knees, Slaughter them despite their pleas. Throw them in the ovens hot, Soap and lampshades sold and bought, Made of the Jews that we shot. Mercy's something I have not. With the bomb and machinegun, Blast at them and watch them run. We will have a lot of fun, Shoot and kill Jews one by one."[88]

Given the picture that emerges of "Asadullah al-Shishani"—a hardcore fanatic volunteering as a manager on elite jihadi web forums, who seeks to assist the Pakistani Taliban in launching attacks on the United States, and who sings gaily about murdering innocent people—one might imagine his real identity is that of a high-ranking al-Qaeda terrorist in Iraq or Afghanistan. In fact, nothing could be further from the case—"Asadullah al-Shishani" is actually 21-year old Penn State college student Emerson Begolly, a native of Pittsburgh. In January 2011, FBI agents finally moved in on Begolly as he sat in a vehicle outside a fast food restaurant in New Bethlehem. When he noticed agents approaching him, Begolly attempted to resist arrest and "allegedly bit the agents, drawing blood." Upon subduing and searching their suspect, the agents recovered a loaded 9mm handgun.[89] Further searches at Begolly's primary residence turned up homemade video recordings of Begolly dressed in camouflage and jihadi gear, armed to the teeth, and apparently practicing would-be military maneuvers.[90]

Curiously, Begolly is neither Chechen, nor did he ever actually visit local mosques or Islamic centers in Pennsylvania. In fact, as far as the Muslim community in Pittsburgh is concerned, Emerson Begolly never existed. His entire indoctrination and radicalization process evidently took place on-line, exclusively via al-Qaeda social networking forums. No amount of eavesdropping or inside sources recruited from within a mosque would have led investigators to Begolly—only his violent ramblings posted on the internet. This is the biggest challenge facing U.S. law enforcement in the coming years. While Begolly might not be capable of launching the next 9/11 all by himself, al-Qaeda doesn't need to achieve that level of success in order to stay relevant. Rather, as pointed out to me by jihadi veteran Abdullah Anas, "in order to spoil things and to stay on the front page of the news and the satellite channels, they don't need much. Just one, from one thousand. If you have one in the list to wear the jacket with the TNT, that is enough."

[84] Gendar, Alison. "Former New Yorker Samir Khan behind graphics of new Al Qaeda recruiting magazine." New York Daily News. July 18, 2010.
[85] "The Ultimate Mowing Machine." Inspire Magazine. Al-Malahem Media Wing; al-Qaeda in the Arabian Peninsula (AQAP). Issue No. 2; Released on October 11, 2010.
[86] http://www.ansar1.info/showthread.php?t=21859. May 3, 2010.
[87] http://www.alqimmah.net/showthread.php?p=17492. June 1, 2010.
[88] http://www.ansar1.info/showthread.php?t=22963. June 3, 2010.
[89] "Natrona Heights man accused of biting FBI agents." Pittsburgh Tribune-Review. January 6, 2011.
[90] http://www.youtube.com/watch?v=7yiHkuud8Yw. May 2011.

46

46

(VI) CONCLUSIONS

Looking back on the tumultuous career of the late Osama bin Laden, it is truly striking how far al-Qaeda has evolved from its humble origins as a tightly-knit cabal largely based in Pashtun regions of Afghanistan into a multi-national enterprise with associate branches across the Muslim world—not to mention a blossoming ideological appeal which propels seemingly-random individuals into taking this battle upon themselves in their own backyard. The killing of Osama bin Laden delivered a striking blow to the morale of this al-Qaeda enterprise, and it has provided perhaps a brief interruption in their operational planning. The substantial intelligence gathered from bin Laden's compound in Abbottabad may yet lead us to the hideouts of further high-ranking al-Qaeda leaders. Moreover, bin Laden's successor—be it Ayman al-Zawahiri or someone else—could prove to be a far less capable leader than Osama. But, ultimately, the terrorist threat faced by America today is multi-faceted and no longer the exclusive product of bin Laden and a handful of dusty terrorist training camps perched along the Afghan-Pakistani border. Thus, whether we speak of al-Qaeda as a centralized organization, a globally-franchised web of affiliates, or simply as an organizing principle guiding homespun radical extremists, it seems quite clear that al-Qaeda will continue to present a serious and undeniable threat to the U.S. homeland for the foreseeable future.

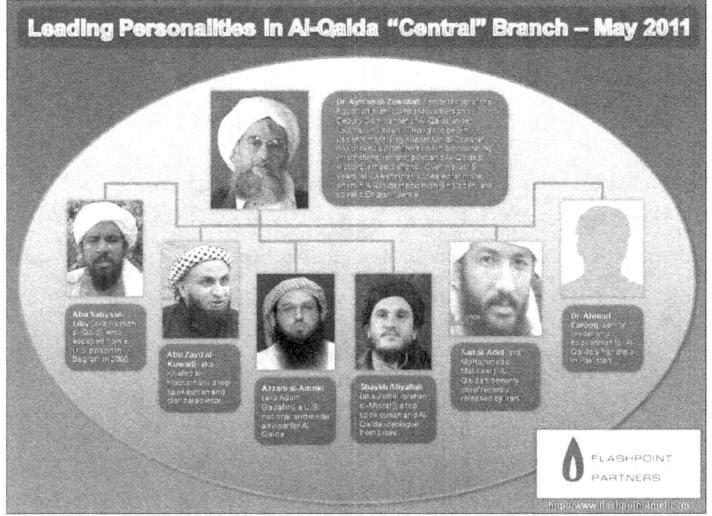

47

Chairman KING. I thank all the witnesses for their testimony.

I will start off the questioning, I guess Mr. Bergen and Mr. Kohlmann first. Both of you have mentioned al-Qaeda in the Arabian Peninsula. They are the one franchise which has shown the most interest in attacking the United States, attacking the homeland. We also have al Shabab, which has recruited at least three dozen Americans. I have heard reports, and can you confirm it at all, that the possibility of a linkup between AQAP and al Shabab and using those combined facilities to attack the mainland, attack the homeland.

Mr. KOHLMANN. Yes. We do have evidence that both al-Qaeda in the Arabian Peninsula and Shabab al-Mujahideen in Somalia are in communication with each other. The communications in fact are not necessarily even secret. About a year and a half ago, Sheik Anwar al-Awlaki, the infamous fugitive Yemeni American cleric who is serving as a spiritual adviser to AQAP-engaged in an open exchange of letters over the web with Shabab al-Mujahideen endorsing their struggle, offering advice and support.

The other thing is that if you pay attention to propaganda put out by AQAP in Yemen, you will notice that a disturbing number of articles and interviews published in their magazine, be it in English or Arabic or other languages, are actually about Somalia, are about Shabab, are about the need to link up. What they have discussed is the idea of actually taking control of the straits leading into the Red Sea, controlling the straits on the Horn of Africa side in the hands of Shabab, and the other side controlled by AQAP, and shutting off shipping through the channel. That may be a grandiose objective, but it gives you an idea of them working together in a partnership in the future.

Chairman KING. The fact that you would have American citizens in al Shabab, it would also give them, I believe, more of an entree to the United States.

Mr. KOHLMANN. That is correct. There are numerous Americans now in both groups. There is Samir Khan, a former resident of Charlotte, North Carolina, and of New York, New York, who is currently serving as a media advisor to al-Qaeda in Yemen, who is the editor behind their infamous *Inspire* magazine. In Somalia, you have individuals such as Omar Hammami, the former Alabama native who has gone over and not only is providing advice to Shabab, but is actually a leader of Shabab; in fact, appeared on camera in the past few days at a Shabab really entitled "We Are All Osama," giving a speech in English indicating that Shabab would be at the forefront of trying to carry out vengeance attacks in the name of bin Laden against the United States.

Chairman KING. Mr. Bergen.

Mr. BERGEN. I would give a minor caveat to that. The Americans who have gone to Somalia to fight, a lot of them have died. It is very dangerous over there.

Second, they are very well-known to the American Government, and some of the gentlemen that Mr. Kohlmann just mentioned are very well-known. I think it is quite unlikely that they come to the United States.

What is much more plausible is they might mount an operation on an American target overseas, say, in Kenya. A lot easier to do.

You don't have the same set of problems of their coming in the no-fly list and all the other things you face in this country.

Chairman KING. A question for Congressman Hamilton and also Ms. Townsend. On the treasure trove of intelligence that has been gathered, we are an instant gratification society, and virtually the day after the intelligence was found, people were asking, what did we find, what did we learn?

Based your experience at the 9/11 Commission and, Fran, your experience in the White House, how long do you think it will take us to have a real analysis of the intelligence that was gathered, considering I think it is well over a million pieces? How long that will it take to get a real analysis of that, and where would that lead?

Ms. TOWNSEND. Mr. Chairman, first you have got to look at what is the total amount of material. Let us take out any analysis related to the pornography that was found. By the way, not a surprising find, not unique to seizures against raids of Taliban and al-Qaeda hideouts in Afghanistan. So it was not at all shocking to me, but it will take up a lot of space in terms of the material.

When you look at then what is remaining, they have got a 24/7, my understanding, capability of sort of triaging it, if you will. You are already seeing some of the things. What they are going to look for are, first and foremost, potential plots, and they will act against those immediately, not waiting to complete the analysis; second, locational data for high-value targets to take advantage of what may be in there, but perishable; and then sort of a broader understanding of the organization, how they communicate and how they operate.

This is going to be an on-going process. I think the one thing we ought to take confidence in is they won't wait to complete it to act on it. They will act on it as they reveal the material.

Chairman KING. Chairman Hamilton.

Mr. HAMILTON. I think by all odds the most important thing is to identify imminent threats to the United States and our allies. So you want to go through the material quickly to see if you can identify immediate threats. I suspect that process has been pretty well completed.

Beyond that, of course, intelligence is a very tedious business, and you look for bits of information from thousands of sources and try to put that information together. That does take time; not just a matter of hours or days, but it takes months and even years to do it. So it is an extremely difficult process, and, of course, all of this is in foreign language and all the rest of it.

I can't predict for you how long it will be before we get benefits from the information that we have. You have to keep in mind that all of the information you want is never in a single source; that is, you have to take this information and compare it with information from other sources, and that takes time, too.

So it is a trove. It is an enormous treasure for us. Will it benefit us? Almost certainly the answer to that is yes. How quickly? I have no idea how quickly it would be. But I think it is a great find and kind of a benefit that perhaps we did not anticipate when we went in to get Osama bin Laden.

Chairman KING. Thank you, Chairman Hamilton.

I recognize the Ranking Member Mr. Thompson.

Mr. THOMPSON. Thank you very much, Mr. Chairman.

I would like unanimous consent to enter into the record the 2011 Grant Program Funding Summary for the House Homeland Security Committee.

Chairman KING. Without objection, so ordered.

[The information follows:]

INFORMATION SUBMITTED FOR THE RECORD BY RANKING MEMBER BENNIE G. THOMPSON

FISCAL YEAR 2011 GRANT PROGRAM FUNDING SUMMARY

Below is a summary of the funding allocations for each program which is compared to fiscal year 2010 funding levels.

- $526 million—State Homeland Security Grant Program (SHSG) will receive a cut of $315 million, which would result in reduced funding for highest risk States due to the mandatory minimums for States in Sec. 2004 of the 9/11 Commission Act of 2007. Each State or territory allocation will be cut between 22 to 50% and the new minimum allocation reduced to $5.1 million, down from $6.6 million in fiscal year 2010.

  Additional "carve-outs" within the SHSG program received the following allotments:

  - *Metropolitan Medical Response System (MMRS).*—$39.3 million—a cut of $4.4 million for fiscal year 2010.
  - *Citizen Corp Program (CCP).*—$12.4 million—a cut of $2.5 million.
  - *Operation Stonegarden (OPSG).*—$60 million—a cut of $5.1 million.
  - *Driver's License Security Grant Program (DLSGP).*—$48 million—a cut of $3 million.

- $10 million—Tribal Homeland Security Grant Program (THSGP) was the only grant program not cut from fiscal year 2010 allocations:

- $681 million—Urban Area Security Initiative (UASI) would receive a cut of $169 million, which would reduce the number of Tier 2 urban areas receiving funding under the UASI program from 64 in fiscal year 2010 to 31 in fiscal year 2011. Tier 1 urban areas represent the top 11 at-risk and will receive level funding from fiscal year 2010. San Diego was moved up to Tier 1. Please see Appendix B for the list of localities funded and those eliminated from the UASI program.

  One additional "carve-out" is within the UASI program:

  - *UASI Nonprofit Security Grant Program (NGSP).*—$19 million—a cut of $38,000 from fiscal year 2010.

- $14.1 million—Emergency Operations Center (EOC) Grant Program receives a 75% cut from its fiscal year 2010 allotment of $57.6 million;

- $14.1 million—Regional Catastrophic Preparedness Grant Program (RCPGP) would receive a cut of $19.4 million;

- $329 million—Emergency Management Performance Grant Program (EMPG) receives on [sic] minor cut of 0.2% or $659,000 for its fiscal year 2010 enacted levels;

- $235 million—Transit Security Grant Program (TSGP) would receive a cut of $32.9 million;

  Additional "carve-outs" within the TSGP program received the following allotments:

  - *Freight Rail Security Grant Program (FRGSP).*—$10 million—a cut of $4.5 million.
  - *Intercity Passenger Rail (Amtrak).*—$19.9 million—a minor cut of $40,000.
  - *Intercity Bus Security Grant Program (IBSGP).*—$4.9 million—a $6.5 million reduction. IBSGP is a new carve-out in fiscal year 2011.

- $235 million—Port Security Grant Program would receive a cut of $52.9 million.

Please Note.—The Buffer Zone Protection Plan (BZPP) grant which assists State and locals to build security and risk-management capabilities and Interoperable Emergency Communications Grant Programs were defunded.

APPROPRIATIONS COMMITTEE RELEASES FISCAL YEAR 2012 HOMELAND SECURITY
APPROPRIATIONS BILL

MAY 12, 2011

Washington, DC.—The House Appropriations Committee today released its proposed fiscal year 2012 Department of Homeland Security (DHS) Appropriations bill. The legislation will be marked-up in subcommittee tomorrow, and is among the first Appropriations bills to move to subcommittee this year.

Given the importance of providing adequate funding for the safety and security of the Nation, as well as the urgent need to reduce spending to rein in the Nation's unprecedented deficits and debt, the legislation makes serious strides to focus funding in areas where it's most needed, while significantly trimming spending elsewhere. Overall, the fiscal year 2012 Homeland Security Appropriations bill provides $40.6 billion in total non-emergency funding for the various programs and agencies within DHS. This is a decrease of $1.1 billion—or 2.6%—below last year's level and $3 billion—or 7%—below the President's request.

Appropriations Chairman Hal Rogers made the following statement on the legislation:

"To address our historic deficit crisis, we must make the most of our limited resources and rein in unnecessary and wasteful spending in virtually every area of Government—including homeland security. The Department's budget has grown at a rapid rate—over 42% since 9/11—and while it is critical that we maintain crucial measures to keep our Nation safe, we must also protect our country from the very real dangers of uncontrolled deficits and debt. This legislation will prioritize funding for frontline operations and programs to uphold the highest level of National security, while trimming back budgets in less essential areas," Chairman Rogers said.

Homeland Security Subcommittee Chairman Robert Aderholt also commented on his bill:

"Homeland security and fiscal discipline are National priorities and the fiscal year 2012 Department of Homeland Security Appropriations bill addresses both," said Chairman Aderholt. "The recent storms that swept the Southeast and the death of Osama bin Laden serve as sobering reminders of our Nation's continued need for robust National security and disaster recovery. The bill recognizes the critical importance of the homeland security mission—fully funding all intelligence and watch listing functions, as well as all frontline personnel. The bill also reflects the unquestioned need for fiscal restraint, reduces spending wherever possible, and prioritizes taxpayers' limited dollars toward the vital security programs that will have an immediate impact on our Nation's safety and security."

Bill Highlights

Savings and Oversight.—The misleading and inadequate budget request from the President for DHS overtly underfunded known disaster relief costs of more than $4.9 billion (requesting only $1.8 billion), relied on $650 million in increased revenue from fees that Congress has not approved, and included undefined and unspecified "administrative savings" of more than $803 million. In contrast, the committee's legislation ignores these accounting gimmicks and provides real budget savings, better efficiency, and stringent oversight of DHS spending while prioritizing disaster response and the frontline operations that most directly and immediately enhance our National security.

The legislation includes major cuts to programs that have underperformed, been ill-managed, or not proven beneficial for the cost. Also, the bill requires numerous expenditure plans from DHS in order to improve its budget justifications and better align funding to tangible security results.

FEMA State and Local Grant Reform.—The bill includes long-overdue reform of the State and Local Grant program under the Federal Emergency Management Agency (FEMA), which has been plagued by inefficiency and has been unable to demonstrate a measurable return on taxpayer investments. These grants often remain in Federal coffers for many years—including a current backlog of over $13 billion in unspent funds. To address these challenges, the bill reduces the total grant funding by $2.1 billion, requires increased measurement, reporting, and oversight of existing funds, and permits the Secretary of DHS to issue grants in a competitive, merit-based process to prioritize areas with the highest risk and greatest need—getting the most out of each and every tax dollar.

Critical Security Operations and Programs.—The committee's legislation prioritizes funding for frontline security operations, including personnel, intelligence activities, and the acquisition of selected essential tactical resources. This includes increasing staffing levels of the Border Patrol, Customs and Border Protection (CBP) field operations, Immigration and Customs Enforcement (ICE), Coast Guard, Secret Service, and other essential security personnel. In addition, the bill fully funds all requested increases for intelligence gathering activities, including "watch listing" and threat identification.

Earmarks.—This bill contains no earmarks, as defined by clause 9(e) of Rule XXI of the House Rules.

U.S. Customs and Border Protection.—The bill contains $11.8 billion for Customs and Border Protection (CBP)—an increase of $443 million over last year's level. This funding provides for a total of 21,370 border patrol agents and 21,186 CBP officers, additional training and canine units at ports of entry, $149 million for Inspection and Detection Technology, and $500 million for Air and Marine operations and procurement. The bill increases funding for CBP's targeting systems by $15 million to enhance the identification of known and suspected terrorists and criminals, and contains a total of $500 million for border security fencing, infrastructure, and technology.

Immigration and Customs Enforcement.—The bill provides $5.8 billion for Immigration and Customs Enforcement (ICE), which is $35 million above last year's level. This includes $1.7 billion for domestic investigation programs, $147 million for international enforcement programs, $81 million for the Office of Intelligence, $32.5 million for the Visa Security Program, and an additional $64 million for continued expansion of the Secure Communities program. In addition, the legislation includes $2.7 billion—an increase of $27 million above the President's request—for ICE detention bed spaces, raising the total number of beds to 34,000, the largest detention capacity in ICE's history.

Transportation Security Administration (TSA).—The bill includes $7.8 billion for the TSA, an increase of $125 million over last year's level, and $293 million below the President's request. These funds will be used to sustain the current cap level of 46,000 full-time screening personnel, and for explosive detection systems, security enforcement, cargo inspections, Federal Air Marshals, and other TSA activities. The bill also includes an additional $10 million to address air cargo threats. However, the bill does not provide $76 million requested by the President for 275 additional advanced inspection technology (AIT) scanners nor the 535 staff requested to operate them.

Coast Guard.—The bill contains $10 billion for the U.S. Coast Guard, which is $196 million below last year's level, and provides funding for maritime safety and security activities, counternarcotics enforcement, facilities and equipment maintenance, and overseas contingency operations including operations in the Persian Gulf. Within the total, the legislation fully sustains military pay and allowances, and provides targeted increases above the budget request for communications, tactical training, and acquisition of critical operations assets such as small boats and replacement helicopters.

Secret Service.—The bill includes $1.7 billion for the U.S. Secret Service—an increase of $155 million over last year's level. This includes $113 million for protective activities related to the 2012 Presidential Election, and $43 million for information technology improvements including cybersecurity and threat assessment capabilities.

Federal Emergency Management Agency.—The bill includes $5.3 billion for FEMA—a decrease of $1.9 billion from last year's level. This total includes a cut of $2.1 billion to State and Local grants (as noted above), and an increase of $850 million to the Disaster Relief Fund (DRF). The bill provides $1 billion for FEMA's State and Local Programs, and includes increased oversight, better prioritization of funding to address critical needs and high-risk areas, and a report on the expenditure of the current $13 billion in backlogged, unexpended grant funds leftover from previous years. The bill fully funds Emergency Management Performance Grants at $350 million and provides $350 million for firefighting grants. To better address the costs of both known and expected disasters, the legislation also includes a total of $2.65 billion for the DRF.

Guantanamo Bay Detention Facility and Detainees.—The legislation includes a provision prohibiting funds to transfer, release, or assist in the transfer or release of Guantanamo detainees to or within the United States or its territories. The provision also prohibits immigration benefits to Khalid Sheikh Mohammed or any other detainee.

Mr. THOMPSON. Again, we have tremendous experience. I would like to kind of put a softball question on you and see how you come back with it.

Given what you know about the threat we face since the death of bin Laden, as well as before, are there some things that you think we as Members of Congress ought to do that we are not doing to keep the threat to the homeland to a minimum?

I will start with you, Congressman.

Mr. HAMILTON. You always have to be careful when somebody says they are throwing you a softball question. It almost invariably means it is going to be hard to answer.

Well, I go back to the basics here. I don't think the homeland security agenda is radically changed because of Osama bin Laden's death. We still have items that we know we must deal with in homeland security that we have not dealt with, and they have been on the agenda for 10 years. I have mentioned the radio spectrum issue, the ability to communicate, and the ability to have unity of command.

But Congress has to get its act together in both intelligence and homeland security. You folks are part of the problem because you haven't put your act together with regard to homeland security oversight and with your intelligence oversight.

So rather than looking far away at a lot of things and trying to come up with new ideas as a result of this dramatic success, I think you have to kind of go back to the basics that have been on the agenda for quite a long period of time. I think what the Chairman said in his opening statement, and I think several of the witnesses mentioned, for 10 years now after 9/11, the American people have moved on to all kinds of other interests and focuses, and so there is a kind of complacency and lack of urgency that sets in.

What can Members of Congress do? I think Members of Congress can emphasize to their constituents again and again that this is still a very serious threat to the United States, and we must not become complacent. These people will find a way to attack us. I have very little doubt that we will be attacked again in the future. We hope not. We have been very fortunate; maybe more than fortunate. We have been very good protecting ourselves. But the threat is still there. So what can you do? You can keep people reminded of the fact that this threat is still alive.

Mr. THOMPSON. Thank you.

Ms. Townsend.

Ms. TOWNSEND. Congressman, I appreciate the question, and I am going to give you three specific things that I think are available for you all to really help with. They are not new, but we haven't adequately addressed them.

What do we know about al-Qaeda's targeting? They are obsessed with the transportation sector of our infrastructure. We have not done enough when it comes to rail security. We still don't have 100 percent of cargo screening despite this threat with the computer cartridges. So renewed emphasis and investment on transportation security, including rail and cargo and infrastructure generally, is very important.

Second, it is about technology. You heard me talk about the need for both the Government investigators and intelligence to have the resources, the capability that they need to not to keep up with the bad guys, but to be ahead of them. Oftentimes, even when they have the technology, the legal authority to actually use it effec-

53

tively lags behind. Of course, Congress can help with that. I would reemphasize, Congressman Hamilton, the need for bandwith for first responders.

Last is the only people who can really effectively address what we call the low-probability, high-consequence event—radiological, nuclear, biological—is the Federal Government. I worry, because we have talked about it but not seen an attack, that we haven't done enough. This is one of these we don't want to think about it because of the horrible consequences, but, in fact, we know from their own statements they are committed to an anthrax capability, they are committed to obtaining nuclear. I worry 10 years after 9/11 that the resources and commitment, whether it is the Strategic National Stockpile or other such programs that help prevent, detect, or respond to such things, are inadequate.

Mr. BERGEN. I would just say that I think it is important for the committee to communicate to the American people that the threat is not just coming from al-Qaeda. When I say the threat, I mean the threat to the domestic American homeland. Pakistani Taliban recruited and trained Faisal Shehzad. The Islamic Jihad unit, which is sort of an Uzbek group, recruited guys to attack Ramstein Air Force Base in 2007. They accumulated 1,600 pounds of hydrogen. That are now operating in an al-Qaeda-like manner.

Mr. KOHLMANN. Thank you, sir. I think that law enforcement in this country has made tremendous leaps and bounds in terms of their evolution since 9/11. But the FBI and Department of Justice are still grappling with some issues relating to virtual sanctuaries. We have gone after al-Qaeda in their physical sanctuaries in places like Afghanistan and Pakistan, but right now there are virtual sanctuaries for al-Qaeda on the internet where al-Qaeda is able to put bomb-making instructions, recruit people, communicate with each other out of the view of the American public.

What most people wouldn't realize is that top-tier al-Qaeda members in Afghanistan on the frontline are chatting with each other over social networking forums that are hosted in western countries by major corporations. That can't go on. So I think one of the roles that the U.S. Congress can play is, No. 1, to put pressure on law enforcement to continue to reform itself, to continue to acquire high-tech tools, which will put the FBI one step ahead of cyber jihadists. I think also, very importantly, is to put pressure on the private corporations that are serving as the unwitting hosts for this material. Obviously, YouTube and Facebook don't want to have anything to do with al-Qaeda. But I think it is time that both of these companies, along with hosts of others that are responsible for hosting al-Qaeda material, make more of an effort than simply try to rely on volunteer efforts by people who are opposed to the message of al-Qaeda, which is what they are doing right now. It is time that these companies take the responsibility of making sure that their resources are not being misused to recruit people like Faisal Shahzad, like Umar Abdulmutallab and push them to join al-Qaeda.

Mr. THOMPSON. Thank you very much. You hit the softball.

I would like, Mr. Chairman, unanimous consent that Mr. Green, former Member of the committee, be allowed to sit for this hearing.

Chairman KING. Mr. Thompson, obviously I will not object. But we are considering charging Mr. Green rent for all the time he spends with us.

Recognize the gentleman from Texas, the Chairman of the Subcommittee on Oversight, Mr. McCaul.

Mr. McCAUL. Thank you, Mr. Chairman. I would like to first take this moment just to publicly commend the Navy SEALs, the intelligence community, particularly the analysts in both NSA and CIA for a job well done in bringing him to justice. They are really the unsung heroes whose names and faces the American people may never know.

With that, this hearing that for us is the impact of al-Qaeda after the killing of Osama bin Laden. There was a debate going on as to where he was located. Was he in a cave? Was he operational? Was he just a figurehead? Most people thought he was more of an inspirational figurehead. From what I have seen, that debate may be changing somewhat.

There were 27 terror plots over the last 2 years. I think my first question is, of those 27, how many of those do you believe may have been inspired by those like al-Awlaki who inspired Major Hasan just north of my district in Fort Hood, and other franchise operations, versus the bin Laden operation? We know with the predator drones that the command and control structure was greatly decentralized and damaged.

So with that, to me, that goes to the core of the question: If you analyze the last 2-year terror plots, how many of those do you believe were actually inspired or motivated by Osama bin Laden?

Mr. KOHLMANN. I would just say this: I work as a consultant on behalf of the FBI, and I evaluate evidence and I serve as an expert witness in terrorism trials here in the United States. I have yet to see a single homegrown terrorism case in the United States that did not include at least some material by Anwar al-Awlaki. His recordings pop up in basically every single homegrown terrorism case that is litigated by the Department of Justice in this country; and, frankly, it appears in every single case outside of this country as well.

That doesn't mean that bin Laden isn't influential, either. His materials show up, too. The difference between bin Laden and al-Awlaki is that al-Awlaki may not have military credentials, but he speaks fluent English, he is extremely charismatic, he is a good speaker, and he has religious credentials which I guess take the place of the military ones. He won't ever replace bin Laden, but he is a tremendously influential figure. There is absolutely no doubt that he continues to radicalize people. People right now, at this very moment, are being arrested in the United States with connections to al-Awlaki, have tried reaching out to al-Awlaki. Very dangerous people.

Mr. McCAUL. Most of these were homegrown radicalization cases inspired by al-Awlaki. Does anybody else on the panel have any comments on that?

Mr. BERGEN. In the U.S. military, there is a document called Commander's Intent, which means that General Petraeus doesn't have to tell a soldier in Kandahar what to do, and bin Laden was in charge of Commander's Intent. So al-Awlaki, the reason he is important in these cases is because he speaks English. It is that simple. If he was speaking in Arabic, he wouldn't be that important. It is not that he is a significant religious figure, or as Mr. Kohlmann said, a significant military figure. It is that he is communicating in colloquial English.

Al-Awlaki is no Osama bin Laden. He can't change the strategic intent of al-Qaeda. At the end of the day, al-Qaeda in the Arabian Peninsula is a branch of al-Qaeda Central, operating to fulfill bin Laden's strategic guidance.

If the new leader of al-Qaeda came along and said we are not going to attack the United States anymore, you know, al-Awlaki would still be out there and he may take a different view. But at the end of the day, al-Awlaki is not in charge of this movement. He is a number—you know, not insignificant leader of a branch of the larger mother ship.

Mr. MCCAUL. I agree with that assessment. I always said the death of bin Laden marked the beginning of the end. Because we couldn't truly win the war on terror until we killed bin Laden. So that is why I believe this is so significant.

Mr. HAMILTON. Mr. McCaul, if I may say so. I don't have a detailed analysis of the 27 that you mentioned, but my answer to the question of how many were inspired by Osama bin Laden would be all of them. He was a symbolic figure, he was an icon, and he had enormous influence here. I can't imagine any of these terrorists striking without paying some homage and allegiance to him. This man was extraordinarily charismatic.

Sitting in the 9/11 Commission listening to testimony, I kept asking myself, how in the world could a man persuade 19 young men to go to their deaths? Now, you talk about persuasive powers. That is persuasive power. I know it is a different environment, a different religion and all the rest of it, but the instinct for self-preservation is pretty strong. He persuaded 19 people to kill themselves. That is the kind of authority and charisma he had, in a very evil way of course. He inspired all of them.

Chairman KING. I will go to another gentleman from Texas, Mr. Cuellar.

Mr. CUELLAR. Thank you very much, Mr. Chairman. I want to thank the witnesses for being here with us.

You know, when somebody comes into the United States, Border Patrol will classify them as Mexicans or OTMs. That is, other than Mexicans. The large number of folks who are coming into the United States are Mexicans coming in for economic reasons. Then after that you have Central Americans, and then you have other folks. Traditionally, that is what the numbers have been with the Border Patrol.

There was a CRS report that said that—and I am quoting: "The sheer increase of non-Mexicans, the OTMs, coming across the border makes it more difficult for United States Border Patrol agents to readily identify and process each OTM, thereby increasing the chance that a potential terrorist could slip into the system. Moreover, there is no reliable data concerning how many OTMs may evade apprehension and successfully enter the country legally across the country."

Then CRS raises a couple of potential issues. One potential issue for Congress is whether to increase in OTM apprehensions poses a threat to National security. Then another potential threat, according to the CRS, for Congress, is the indication that hundreds of people that come from countries known to harbor terrorists or to promote terrorism are caught trying to enter into the United States illegally across the land border.

If you look at the handout out there, and this is OTMs, the OTM members, you should have a handout before you. This is not Mexicans. This is OTMs. The large number of them are coming in from Central America, 22,360. This is for fiscal year 2011. Then you have India, and then you have South America. By South America, you are talking about all the countries of South America. Then China. Then Romania.

The second handout deals with just focusing not on the Mexicans or the Central Americans, but this is the rest of the OTMs. India in the fiscal year 2011 had 1,662, more than the 1,660, which includes all of South America. Every country put together came in from there. Then you have China, and then you have Romania.

Now, my question is, what sort of issues does this bring up?

Keep in mind, I think you might be familiar, India and Guatemala, I think it was back in 2009, entered into some sort of agreement where they have a non-visa, or waiver of visas, going into Guatemala. So maybe that is a pipeline that just gets them coming in, like Brazil did some years ago.

But my question is, when you have folks coming in from, let's say, India and the area that they come, what sort of potential issues does this bring when we talk about threats to the United States, if any? To any of the panelists.

Ms. TOWNSEND. Seeing no one else step up to this one. Congressman, this has been, as I am sure you know, during my time in the Bush administration, I was a vocal advocate for comprehensive immigration reform. I view comprehensive immigration reform as a necessary, fundamentally necessary thing to protect our National security.

During my time in the Government, there had been some intelligence to suggest that al-Qaeda looked at this pipeline coming across the U.S.-Mexican border. I will leave the politics to those of you for whom it is a profession, and say to you that I believe that the lack of comprehensive immigration reform is a vulnerability. I would prefer to see, as it was true in my time in Government, to have the Border Patrol and the Immigration Service focus their resources on people who are going to do us harm.

That does not mean I think we don't have to address the phenomenon of illegal immigration in a fundamentally fair and basic dignified way, but I believe that we need comprehensive reform.

Mr. HAMILTON. May I just add my word in support of comprehensive immigration reform. We have to begin to look at immigration through the prisms of both the National economy. We need a lot of people at the top of the skill level and at the bottom. We have to begin to look at immigration as a National security matter as well. That means quite a change of perspective on immigration for what we have had in years past.

At the border, you would know more than I, but I think we have increased our manpower doubling it over a period of a few years, the number of Border Patrol agents. I think we have made substantial progress in letting illegal people into the country. Obviously, we have to continue that for a long time to come. We have still got to deploy a lot better technology. We have got to get better on this US–VISIT exit system that I mentioned in my testimony today. So there are a lot of things that I think still need to be done.

But I very much agree with Fran's observation about comprehensive reform. You cannot deal with immigration on a piecemeal basis. You cannot do it.

Chairman KING. The time of the gentleman expired. Would the gentleman ask unanimous consent to have his exhibits placed into the record?

Mr. CUELLAR. Yes, I do. Thank you.

Chairman KING. Without objection.

[The information follows:]

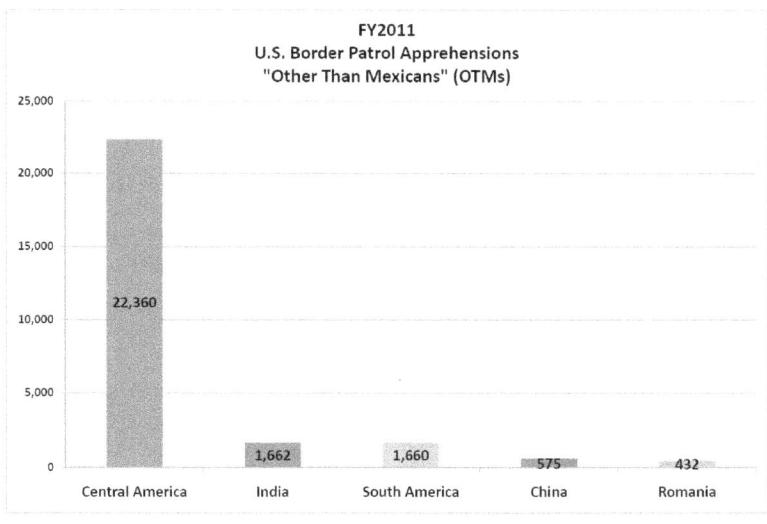

 Prepared by the Office of Congressman Henry Cuellar

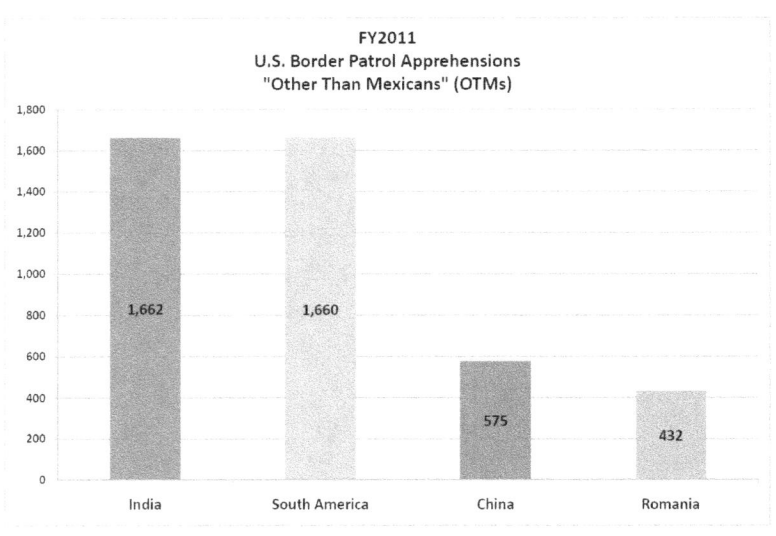

FY2011
U.S. Border Patrol Apprehensions
"Other Than Mexicans" (OTMs)

Prepared by the Office of Congressman Henry Cuellar

Chairman KING. Also, before I recognize the next questioner, I think we ought to acknowledge the fact that Mr. Long is not here today; that he represents Joplin, Missouri, where they lost so many lives and so much property. So all of our thoughts and prayers are with Congressman Long today.

With that, I recognize for 5 minutes the distinguished gentleman, Dr. Broun, from Georgia.

Mr. BROUN. Thank you, Mr. Chairman.

This morning on "Washington Journal" on C–SPAN, I had referred to this hearing as a huddle between decisionmakers and the experts so that we can come up with a game plan of where we go from here. I appreciate you all being here. I appreciate your valuable testimony. I agree with the Chairman, it is absolutely essential that the American public not become complacent. I think we have, Mr. Chairman, become complacent in very many ways.

I had a number of callers talk about various things that and even just dismissed the potential of al-Qaeda or other entities being a danger to this country. I think it is absolutely critical that the American public understand that we have a clear and present danger. So I appreciate you all being here to talk about that.

Now, I worry about the line of succession that the elimination of bin Laden has put in place. Also, the current climate within al-Qaeda poses numerous concerns, most regarding the internal power struggle not only within al-Qaeda, but the associated groups.

Mr. Kohlmann talked about some of the al-Qaeda central people and al-Zawahiri as possibly being the successor to bin Laden. I would like to hear from the other members of the panel about who you all think might replace bin Laden as being the central figure, and also whether the associated groups, AQAP and the leadership there and the other entities, how do you all see this sorting out? What can we do as Members of Congress and what can Government do as we see this power struggle within the al-Qaeda and al-Qaeda AP and other associated groups?

Mr. HAMILTON. Dr. Broun, I believe that al-Qaeda is now searching for another leader. I think the most likely leader, so far as I know, and I yield to other members of the panel here who may know more about it than I. But I think the most likely is Zawahiri is probably going to be the last man standing in the struggle. I think there are internal differences within al-Qaeda. I don't think we should underestimate him. He is ruthless, he is a religious zealot much like Osama bin Laden. He is not a lightweight. He has been instrumental in al-Qaeda's strategy, its development, its evolution over a period of time. I think it would be a very grave mistake to think that, with the removal of Osama bin Laden, they will be led by a feckless leader.

So I think if the American intelligence community now will be spending an enormous time trying to answer your question as to who emerges. But from where I sit, he is the most likely guy to emerge, and we must not underestimate him.

Ms. TOWNSEND. Congressman, I agree with that. I think one of the key things to watch, there has always been a tension about leadership residing with the Egyptians because of just historical differences that I will leave to Peter to discuss. But the fact that Zawahiri and Saif al-Adel, the interim leaders, are both Egyptians suggests that there will continue to be this tension, this struggle between the Egyptian members and the Gulf Arab members. So what that posits is continuing tension between, or some increasing tension, between al-Qaeda central and their affiliates, the strongest of which you have heard us talk about today, al-Qaeda in the Arabian Peninsula.

It reminds me of the tension we saw between al-Qaeda core when that was bin Laden, and another affiliate, al-Qaeda in Iraq, which was Zarqawi. Intelligence was replete with examples of an on-going tension about vision. Zarqawi was a very strong personality. He pushed back on al-Qaeda central. It was a bonanza of targeting opportunity, and we all know Zarqawi wound up targeted and killed as a result of it.

One would hope that al-Awlaki, feeling an opportunity here to push back, that there will be this increasing tension between Zawahiri and what remains of the al-Qaeda core and the affiliate al-Qaeda in the Arabian Peninsula. Because if that tension increases, it provides a tremendous opportunity for the U.S. Government.

Mr. BERGEN. I totally agree with what Representative Hamilton and Fran Townsend have just said, and I would add one minor additional note.

Bin Laden was from Saudi Arabia. As you know, his family is from Yemen. For religiously zealot people inside of al-Qaeda, that is very significant because of the Holy Land, and they want—the reason it is controversial to have an Egyptian is not simply because there are disputes about strategy and targeting; at the end of the day, the Egyptians really want to just have kind of a Taliban-style government in Egypt. They are less interested in attacking the United States. It is also about the idea of having somebody from the Holy Land.

So I think there actually, as Fran has outlined, some real opportunities for the intelligence community and the U.S. Government to kind of be aware of the fractures that are going to develop, and perhaps even exploit them if there are opportunities.

Mr. KOHLMANN. If I might quickly add. Towards your second question about AQAP, about what can be done about AQAP, I think the answer to that goes back to a comment that was made by Anwar al-Awlaki, of all people, recently.

Al-Awlaki pointed to the current wave of instability in Yemen. He laughed and he said, of course this is going to accrue to our benefit. Of course this is going to accrue to al-Qaeda's benefit.

I think that gives you the answer, which is that if you want to damage AQAP, the answer is not just drone strikes, it is not just U.S. special forces operations. A large part of this is contingent upon stability returning to Yemen. Political stability and stability that involves the tribes. Because right now it is the tribes that are providing protection to people like Anwar al-Awlaki, Qassim al-Rimi, the leaders of AQAP. They are being hidden by Yemenis, and you have got to convince them that it is not in their interests to work with al-Qaeda. Right now there are large swaths of central Yemen that are outside of government control. It is the exact nightmare scenario that we have been trying to avoid in Afghanistan and Pakistan, and it is writ-large in the heart of the Middle East.

Mr. BROUN. Thank you, Mr. Chairman. I will yield back.

Chairman KING. I would advise the Members, I understand that Chairman Hamilton will have to leave at 11:45 and Ms. Townsend at 12 noon. So I would ask Members to try to keep it within 5 minutes or phrase their question in a way that allows for a 5-minute answer.

The gentlelady from Texas, Ms. Jackson Lee.

Ms. JACKSON LEE. Thank you very much, Mr. Chairman. To all of the witnesses, let me thank you for your service. I might want to join you, Ms. Townsend, in offering our deepest sympathy to our friends and neighbors and fellow Americans. It seems that it is an unending attack of tornados in the Midwest. But our deepest sympathy to them.

Again, in Homeland Security, thank all of you for confirming the significance of the demise of Osama bin Laden as well as the intelligence.

I want to thank my Chairman, and I hope that will allow me to be able to get 2 or 3 or 4 or 5 minutes after the red light comes on.

Chairman KING. As much as I would love to do that.

Ms. JACKSON LEE. I want to thank him. He has been consistent, along with my Ranking Member, on the focus, Mr. Hamilton, Chairman Hamilton, as that you said. We have got to get our act together. We have got to synergize, integrate the oversight of Homeland Security with all the other agencies that are doing so.

So I might mention to my Chairman that I have introduced H.R. 1900, the Surface Transportation and Mass Transit Security Act. We did it last year with bipartisan support. I frankly, if I might,

I was getting ready to say, I might, stay up nights because I serve as the Ranking Member on the Transportation Security about the vulnerabilities of our rail system, Federal air marshals and utilization of them on many of our flights, and the whole issue of air traffic controllers, though they may have challenges sleeping, if you will, that is part of our security. Many people don't remember how air traffic controllers were so intimately involved on 9/11.

So let me just pose these questions which are related but yet not. That is, help us understand this fascination with transportation, but also rail. In fact, I just want to stick on rail. Most of the times we hear our communities saying I don't want hazardous materials coming through, their fear of various incidents that may impact them, explosions, et cetera. But our rail system, both what it transports along with people I believe is a serious concern. I would appreciate comment about us really focusing on rail security as the 9/11 Commission suggested.

Then finally, my second question is, I co-chair the Pakistan Caucus, have gone to Pakistan on a number of occasions. Pierce into the Taliban, the Taliban of Afghanistan, the Taliban of Pakistan. Do they leap to the United States? Do they continue to terrorize the Pakistani people? You are right, I am amazed at the attack on police and the ability to get on rank-and-file but as well the hierarchy of the Pakistani military. Do we give them the money? Do we give them the social justice money? Where will they take their terror? Will it come to the United States? Chairman Hamilton, if you can go down. Hopefully I will get to all of you.

Thank you, Mr. Chairman.

Mr. HAMILTON. Well, I think on the first point the fascination with rail transportation goes back to the fundamental intent of al-Qaeda.

Look, they are very sophisticated people. They understand symbolic targets. They understand where Americans congregate. They understand how best to disrupt. The transportation of the United States has enormous vulnerabilities. Rail, certainly. But other forms, too.

So I attribute their fascination with it to, No. 1, their skill, I guess, in analyzing our vulnerabilities; and, No. 2, their desire to kill as many Americans as possible and to disrupt American life as much as possible.

On the second question, you were raising the question about Pakistan?

Ms. JACKSON LEE. Well, do the Taliban translate to attack on the United States?

Mr. HAMILTON. I think I will yield to the others on that question.

Ms. TOWNSEND. Yes, ma'am. Look, the obsession with transportation, as you pointed out, is writ-large. We saw the tragedy of using aircraft. But trains represent a real opportunity for them. By the way, also ferries. I mention that, because as the Chairman knows, ferries are very big in terms of transportation into Manhattan in the morning at rush hour.

But back to rail. We saw the attacks in London and Madrid. We know that they continue, if nothing else, because of the Zazi Najibullah case against the New York City subways. They are not going to stop. It represents, because it is an open system—of course, if you close it, it loses its effectiveness in a place like an urban area like New York. But its open system represents its vulnerability. The New York City Police Department has done a tremendous job with sort of unpredictable presence in different subways. None of that is 100 percent. But I really think this goes back to when we talk about the grant program—and I have not always been a huge fan of the Homeland Security grant program. But this is a place where we can actually incentivize State and local authorities to take ownership of this issue and spend their money in a place that really matters not just in the locality but writ-large.

Evan Kohlmann mentioned the priority of attacking our economy. What better way than to attack our transportation system?

The Pakistan Taliban does represent a direct threat to the United States. We saw the Times Square attempted bombing, and they made threats. I think we have got to learn to take these terrorist groups at face value. They may not have tremendous capability, but they have enough to come here and kill Americans.

Mr. BERGEN. Just to add to that point. A canary in the mine on the Pakistani Taliban is they sent suicide bombers to Barcelona in January 2008, and that is according to both themselves and Spanish prosecutors. We should have taken, as Fran—sometimes when people say that, we should take these threats seriously. They, of course, also did a joint operation in Khost that killed the 7 CIA employees and contractors.

What to do about Pakistan is obviously an enormous question before many of the Members here. It is a very complex relationship, and it would be very tempting perhaps to say, well, we are just going to cut off aid. This would be psychologically satisfying for about a week. At the end of the day, they are the fifth-largest country in the world, about to be, with nuclear weapons, headquarters of al-Qaeda and the Taliban, and we need them.

Just one final point on this. More Pakistani soldiers have died fighting the Taliban than U.S. and NATO soldiers combined, and this is just something that is very important for us to recognize and understand when we talk to them and when we think about how to deal with them.

Mr. HAMILTON. I might just add that if you are getting into the U.S.-Pakistan relationship, this is already one of the most difficult bilateral relationships in the world. We are not going to solve the problems in this relationship. We just have to manage them. There are so many voices I have heard coming out of Capitol Hill to cut aid to Pakistan. I would be very, very careful about that.

We have enormous interests in Pakistan. We have referred to them already here this morning: The nuclear weapons. We use Pakistan to transit much of our materials and people going into Afghanistan. The nuclear weapons, of course, are huge.

In the end, we have to focus on the long-term interests of the United States and not our short-term frustration. There are plenty of reasons to be frustrated with the relationship now, but that long-term relationship remains very valuable to us. I think it remains valuable to the Pakistanis as well. All kinds of problems in it, all kinds of questions arise. Sometimes I think Admiral Mullen, the chairman of the Chief of Staff, has been commuting to Pakistan. He goes over there so frequently to try to work out these problems.

63

It just indicates the delicate nature of the relationship. It is a very difficult one, but we have got to work through it.

Mr. KOHLMANN. If I can just very quickly comment about the Pakistani Taliban. My company has an office in Pakistan. One of the subjects we spend most time on is the Pakistani Taliban. We have been interviewing them in recent days. We have been polling them in their opinions.

I can tell you this: No. 1, the Pakistani Taliban is far more sophisticated than people give them credit for. They are recruiting people right now, Americans, using YouTube. They have not done this once, they have done this multiple times. They are recruiting people using Facebook. They are deliberately trying to come up with terrorist plots targeting the United States. They are aggressively trying to target the United States. Perhaps most disturbingly, unlike the Afghan Taliban, the Pakistani Taliban are forging very close relationships with al-Qaeda, with Arab Afghan al-Qaeda militants, to the point where as has just been suggested by Peter Bergen and I believe others, that the Camp Chapman attack that took place in 2009, there is a substantial degree of evidence indicating both the Pakistani Taliban and the Haqqani network played a direct role in that attack.

It raises a lot of questions. It raises questions both about the Pakistani Taliban and their reach into the United States. It also reaches the inevitable question about what is the relationship between the Pakistani Taliban, the Haqqani network, and the ISI, the Pakistani Intelligence Service. Those questions have yet to be fully resolved. But as long as you have terrorist attacks being directed at U.S. targets, including U.S. civilians, by a group that might have ties to the Pakistani Intelligence Service, I think it is worthy to look into those questions and resolve them. Because as much as Pakistan is a critical partner, I don't think we can allow terrorist groups to establish bases with the say-so of the ISI.

Chairman KING. The gentleman from Minnesota, Mr. Cravaack, is recognized for 5 minutes.

Mr. CRAVAACK. Thank you, Mr. Chairman. Thank you very much for being here today. This has been quite enlightening. So thank you for your comments.

First off, being a retired Navy captain, if you focus on the current war, you are missing it altogether. We need to focus on the next war. What we are seeing now, as Mr. Kohlmann—cyber jihadists, I truly feel the previous notion of asymmetric warfare, we have gone way beyond that into something, a new realm, a new difference of what we are actually seeing today.

Ms. Townsend, also we are at a war without borders, and I very much appreciate your comments regarding the lone wolf. In quickly reviewing your background, I would like you to comment a little bit on that, because one of the votes we will be taking very soon is regarding three components of the PATRIOT Act. I was wondering if you could comment on that, if you believe that these are necessary vehicles to make sure that we can protect Americans within the United States without jeopardizing any Constitutional rights that American citizens would have.

Ms. TOWNSEND. As you know, Congressman, the lone wolf represents the greatest challenge to Federal investigators and local authorities. It is unpredictable, it is difficult to identify in advance, unlike an organization where people have got to talk to one another and plan. So I believe that those provisions in the Patriot Act are essential to the FBI's continued ability to effectively do these investigations and identify the threats.

To the extent—I can tell you during my time in the White House when there was the initial renewal of the PATRIOT Act. To the extent there are concerns, there are procedural mechanisms for oversight and reporting that ought to give people the confidence and the courage to vote to extend the PATRIOT Act.

Mr. CRAVAACK. Mr. Hamilton.

Mr. HAMILTON. I support the provisions in the PATRIOT Act as well, and I think they should be extended. Now, obviously, what has happened since 9/11 is the power of the Government has expanded dramatically in terms of intrusion into the lives of people. For necessary reasons, I think all of us have supported that expansion of power. These provisions, I think, Fran, I am correct in saying, just kind of bring you up to date in terms of your ability to keep track of these bad guys.

Having said all of that, may I also put in a plug for the Privacy and Oversight Board, because I think that what you have had over the period of the last decade is this environment in which the security people win every argument, and for obvious reasons, because we are very deeply concerned about our security. But there is not a sufficient pushback on the side of the civil liberties and privacy. That voice needs to be strengthened, I think, within Government across the board, and especially with regard to the intelligence agencies.

So I want a strong PATRIOT Act, but I also want a counterbalance to that with a Privacy and Oversight Board, and I want the President to get that thing up and moving.

Mr. CRAVAACK. Thank you, sir. I appreciate it.

Mr. Bergen, in your testimony, you stated that Pakistan Taliban in the tribal regions has been successful in attempts to attract Western and American recruits and poses a threat to Americans. Obviously, how much cooperation of the Pakistani ISI are you seeing? Do you think that the relationships can be salvaged moving forward?

Mr. BERGEN. I think, Representative Hamilton, I was surprised when he said one of the wisest things possible about this, which is: We are not going to solve our relationship with Pakistan; we are going to have to manage it.

As a point of information, four ISI buildings have been attacked by the Taliban. So the ISI has a very complex relationship with the Taliban.

Are we getting what we want from them? No. Is the Pakistan government doing quite a lot? Yes. Serious military operation in Southern Waziristan in 2009 unlike previous operations, serious operation in SWAT in 2009 as well.

So the enemy of the perfect is not the reasonably okay. What we are seeing right now is I think overall reasonably okay. Could it be better? Yes. Will it get better? I am not sure.

Mr. CRAVAACK. I appreciate your comments and the amount of soldiers that have been killed in action against the Taliban. That was quite telling.

Sir, I have 21 seconds left. So I yield back.

Chairman KING. I thank the gentleman for his prudence. With that, I am pleased to recognize the gentleman from Michigan, Mr. Clarke.

Mr. CLARKE of Michigan. I appreciate all of your collective testimony. It is apparent that Osama bin Laden was a key figure in global terrorism. His death has dealt a severe blow to al-Qaeda. But the terrorist threat to our country still remains, but it increasingly is coming from within the United States.

I represent metropolitan Detroit, the Detroit sector border. Many times our first responders, local police, and fire still can't communicate with their Federal counterparts or their Canadian counterparts. Many of you have mentioned the issue of interoperable communications and how that is going to be important for us to be able to help address this terrorist threat. We currently have a situation where our radios can't talk to each other.

Now, I do thank the Department for releasing prior allocated money, $4 million to Wayne County recently. That will help us upgrade our radio system. But even still, our State and local authorities don't have the revenue to provide their resources and equipment for our first responders. Even in the proposed 2012 budget for this very Department, it is the Homeland Security grants that have been proposed to be cut by, I believe, $2.1 billion compared to 2011 levels.

So all of this begs this question then: How do we best prepare ourselves to deal with the threat of terrorism that comes from within the United States? Where do we get the money? Many have raised that the death of bin Laden poses the opportunity to reassess our National security goals. My point and my question is this: That the assessment could also involve reevaluating our mission in Afghanistan to redirect a part of our military aid that is currently going to Afghanistan, a total of over $100 billion this current year, and to redirect some of that back to the United States to homeland security to protect ourselves from the threat that is increasingly coming from within the United States. If any of you have any comments on how we can best do that. Reassess our mission in Afghanistan. Use some of the money that we are, I was going to say spending, but it is more accurate that we are borrowing, to invest in the military operations in Afghanistan, and to better invest a small portion of that to this budget, the homeland security budget, as a way of better protecting the American people at home by investing those funds right here at home.

Mr. HAMILTON. Congressman, I believe your priority is the correct one. That is to say, we have got to get the ability to communicate at the scene of the disaster. That is so fundamental and so basic. I don't see how it can be argued against.

Now, your question relates to, where do you get the money to do it? I am not an expert on the Federal budget. It involves a lot of questions, what money is in the pipeline that is not being used, for example, that might be available.

You raised the question of Afghanistan. My own personal view with regard to that is that the American people are putting Afghanistan and Iraq in the rearview mirror, and they have already made up their mind pretty much that the United States should begin to withdraw. I don't think the question today is whether or not you should pack up and leave. That is not going to happen nor should it. I don't think the question is whether you are going to achieve victory in Afghanistan. Victory is very hard to define and I don't think that is in the cards. I think American policy increasingly will focus on the question of: What pace do we withdraw from Afghanistan? That will create some funds obviously there. But it is not clear that you can take those funds and immediately put it in some domestic priority.

The question also is that as we withdraw our forces there—this may sound contradictory, but I don't think it is—how can we continue to help Afghanistan to achieve some of the goals that we have a stable Afghanistan obviously is more in our interest than one that is chaotic.

So I think there is a renewed interest in this, and I think the operational question on policy is really the pace of withdrawal at this point. Will it create some funds? Yes, I think it will. That is probably a good thing. But that doesn't necessarily mean you can take those funds and put it into the question of communication.

The question of communication at the scene of the disaster is a highest priority. If you cannot communicate at the scene of the disaster, people lose their lives as happened in New York, as happened in Katrina. This is a priority concern. This is money that has to be found in order to solve this problem. It is frustrating to me beyond measure that 10 years after 9/11 this obvious priority has not been fully met. I know some progress has been made, I know some money has been made available. But we are still not at the point where you can get a seamless communication at the scene of the disaster, which is absolutely what is necessary.

Ms. TOWNSEND. Let me only add, I agree wholeheartedly and enthusiastically with what Congressman Hamilton said. Certainly, if he is not an expert in the Federal budget, I am far behind him.

So, one, I think we can precipitously withdraw from Afghanistan, as the Congressman said. I think as we begin to withdraw down, you are going to find there are additional funds available.

Let me make what I think is an unpopular observation. The responsibility, while heavy on the Federal Government, to solve this problem, and as the Congressman said, it should have been solved by now, it is not unique to the Federal Government. My concern— I mentioned earlier about grant programs. My concern about grant programs is that what happens is the States then abrogate their own responsibility to set aside funds, to make investments in these sorts of things because they rely heavily on the Federal Government.

Frankly, it is clear across the country during this time of fiscal stress that States have not responsibly managed their own budgets. Frankly, I do think that this has got to be a priority not only for the Federal Government but with governors when they are looking at their own State budgets.

Mr. HAMILTON. The homeland security program ought not to be a revenue-sharing program. We recommend that you are not just handing out money to State and local governments. They need money for all kinds of things, some of which are valid and some of which are not. But I think one of the positive things is that in the appropriators' bill, they award grants without regard to the minimum allocations to lower-risk areas. In other words, they followed through on one of the recommendations of the 9/11 Commission, which is to allocate funds on the basis of risk, not just hand out the money everywhere. There are certain areas of the country. New York City is one, but there are others, that are far—Detroit, far higher risk than rural Indiana where I come from. So you have got to make sure that there is enough discretion in the Federal to allocate funds on the basis of risk. This is not a revenue-sharing program.

Chairman KING. The time of the gentleman is expired. I now recognize the gentleman from Pennsylvania, former United States Attorney, Mr. Meehan.

Mr. MEEHAN. I thank you, Mr. Chairman. Thank you to this very distinguished panel for your preparation and your testimony here today.

I am going to ask Ms. Townsend and Mr. Bergen, both of you had commented on something I would like to follow up a little bit on. Ms. Townsend, my experience as a former Federal prosecutor, there is almost a counterintuitive sense that when you take down an organization, either organized crime or even a violent drug gang, it is in the aftermath of that that you see some of the greatest—it is not just a succession thing, but some of the greatest disarray as they reassemble themselves often in terms of violence. You both looked at this as almost a point of opportunity.

What should we be looking for and what opportunities do they actually present in the aftermath of the taking down of Osama bin Laden and the subsequent attempts to try to reorganize?

Ms. TOWNSEND. This is a critical time. I mentioned in my testimony the targeting opportunities. While we won't know publicly what was in the compound, this is a time when they will have to talk to one another. There was reports in the Pakistani media about this meeting that led to the interim leader being appointed the head of the Taliban, Saif al-Adel. How can such a meeting take place when our Pakistani allies are not providing us with targeting information? That would have been a gold mine opportunity to have taken advantage of. But that is what our military and intelligence community are focused on right now.

They are in disarray. They will have to have discussions, meetings in order to resolve their chaos. So all those represent tremendous opportunities, and that is where you want to focus your immediate military resources.

Now, it will be interesting to see whether or not this chaos then permeates out into the affiliates, because right now they represent, as far as I am concerned, the most immediate deadly threat to us, particularly al-Qaeda in the Arabian Peninsula. But we need strong allies. Make no mistake. We have a world-class intelligence community and military capability, but they need real partners.

We have not had very good partners—a real partner in Yemen in President Saleh, and we have a very uncertain partner in Pakistan.

We need to look at ways to how do we—you know, the Congressman said manage the Pakistan relationship. That is right. But they need to produce. It is not that we can walk away from them. They need to produce like a partner produces in terms of targeting capability.

Mr. MEEHAN. Mr. Bergen.

Mr. BERGEN. I don't have anything to add to that.

Mr. MEEHAN. Thank you. Congressman Hamilton, I, as many in this Nation, am tremendously appreciative for the work that you have put into this effort since September 11. You have looked at a lot of different elements. But I noticed twice today in your testimony you focused on this issue of the VISIT exit system. Can you tell me a little bit more about why that is important to you and why you think that is relevant to our protection of the homeland?

Mr. HAMILTON. You just have to keep track of these people when they come into the country. I think the easy thing to do—we lose track of it. It is a difficult thing to do. Seeking a biometric exit system I understand is expensive and has a lot of problems in it, but I think we have just put it off far too long.

It is not just a question of catching these people and stopping it at the border. Some of these people are going to get in. Once you have people in here illegally, or even legally under restricted time limits, you have to be able to keep track of them. That is why you need an exit system as well as an entry system. So it is a real vulnerability in our system to say, okay, we are going to catch these people at the border. Everybody is for that. We don't want the bad guys coming in; but if they do get in just forget about them. You can't do that. You have got to keep track of them. That is what the exit system is all about.

Mr. MEEHAN. Mr. Kohlmann, thank you for your testimony. You identified the world on the internet and the communications that are taking place there. In a free society, it is difficult to try to limit activity on that, but you have given some thought to this. How can we take advantage? In light of both Ms. Townsend testified to about the current moment in which wouldn't we want to be able to have them operating in such a way that we would be able to at least have access to the platform that they are using for communications as a means to have a potential ability to influence their activities?

Mr. KOHLMANN. Yes. I have often said that terrorist websites are like the spy satellite that we never launched. If we are diligent about it, these websites, these forums allow us to monitor the communications taking place at a ground level amongst both al-Qaeda's lieutenants, its supporters, its would-be supporters, people in the West. Increasingly we are seeing individuals who are popping up who were not recruited by any individual or any individual cleric or any individual mosque. They are being motivated purely by what they see on the web. I think, though, I think you are right. I think part of it is we have to keep our eyes on this.

The concern right now is that we are allowing these websites to operate. It is not entirely clear that all elements of our law enforcement and intelligence agencies are aware of what is going on in there. I can tell you only this through personal experience and through the fact that we have an instance where we can point to directly, Fort Hood, where we had a known individual who was infamous as being a recruiter for al-Qaeda and extremist groups, Sheikh Anwar al-Awlaki, who was in open communication with an individual who was a U.S. military serviceman. Those communications, from what I understand, were not entirely innocent or benign.

That is a warning sign. It is a warning sign that as much as this information can provide tremendous clues, if we allow this to proliferate unmonitored, we are giving these folks virtual sanctuary to do whatever the hell they want. That is very worrying.

So it is fine to keep these websites and these forums on-line as long as we are closely monitoring them and tracking the people that are using them, obviously without violating freedom of speech. But the folks that are on the there are dangerous. It is not just computer nerds. The people that are on these forums include bomb makers, include top-ranking Yemeni al-Qaeda operatives, include recruiters for Pakistani Taliban. So we really have to make sure that the FBI and other Government agencies are really watching what is taking place.

Chairman KING. The time of the gentleman has expired. The gentlelady from New York, Ms. Clarke, is recognized for 5 minutes.

Ms. CLARKE of Michigan. Thank you very much, Mr. Chairman, and thank you Ranking Member Thompson. To the panelists, great insight and illumination of the challenges we face.

I am pleased with the discourse of this hearing, because it is important to point out that we must harden our posture of vigilance in keeping our Nation safe in the fight against al-Qaeda and other declared and undeclared terrorist organizations and individuals.

On behalf of the people of the 11th Congressional District of New York, we are really grateful to the Obama administration's leadership, the U.S. military, the CIA intelligence and counterterrorism professionals who carried out that heroic operation to get bin Laden. I would like to say that, as a Member of the committee, it is important to point out that we must continue to remain vigilant. As New Yorkers, I think, unlike maybe other parts of the Nation, are very sensitive, extremely sensitive. I think we are doing very well in terms of our posture of vigilance and awareness in the public. But I think that perhaps one of the things that we can do is get some public service announcements rolling that is aired Nationally, to get people into the understanding of see something, say something, which is something we live with in New York City. So again, I want to thank you for your insightful discussion today.

Bin Laden was an iconic figure of global terrorism. He has inspired militants across the world to commit acts of violence. I wanted to ask, just generally speaking, there is some concern that perhaps at the end of the 40-day mourning period, that many or some Muslims practice that maybe we might see an uptick.

Is there any indication of that? Does 40 days mean anything? I think it is important that if there is mythology out there, we try to get so many plain understanding. I believe we can be hit at any moment. But for those out there who are looking for an indication, would you shed some light on that?

Ms. TOWNSEND. I am happy to take the first shot at this.

Congresswoman, let's be clear. As you know, al-Qaeda and those who subscribe to the ideology are not observant Muslims. These are not real Muslims. So we have already seen what have been called retribution attacks inside Pakistan, whether it is against their military, their police. So those people in the Pakistan Taliban, for example, are not observing any 40-day mourning period.

This is my experience with al-Qaeda, has been they attack when they have the capability and they are positioned to do it, and they will not be, I suspect, constrained by any religious observance.

Mr. KOHLMANN. I would echo. I think it is mythology. I think al-Qaeda will strike when they have the capability to do so. I believe they will try to carry out some kind of revenge attack for the death of bin Laden. But I think it is more likely in the short term that we see something like that against U.S. interests in Pakistan as opposed to inside the United States.

Ms. CLARKE of Michigan. I am glad that you pointed that out. I don't want people to have a false sense of, well, timing. Right? It is important that we are vigilant every moment of every day.

Mr. Kohlmann, I wanted to ask you about threats to water facilities. You know, last Congress the House approved legislation to regulate water and wastewater facilities for security. In your testimony, you described the on-line chatter of various extremists after bin Laden's death and how some of them openly discuss targeted hydroelectric dams, nuclear water plants, and water purification facilities to cause damage to the U.S. economy. Can you elaborate on the threat to critical infrastructure? More specifically, can you articulate what concerns, if any, you have about the terrorist threat to U.S. water facilities, especially given how essential these facilities are to our communities?

Mr. KOHLMANN. In fact, the particular section that you are referring to in my report, the individual specified saying it is not even necessary to poison the water supplies because potentially there are other Islamists out there who might drink this and die. The idea is to create panic, to create terror, to create an urban environment where people are afraid to consume water whether or not there is actually anything wrong with it.

That is the point here, is al-Qaeda is not looking just—again, they are not looking just to kill one American here or there. That is fine to keep them in the headlines. Ultimately, these folks, whether you are talking about the central leadership, the affiliates or the homegrown guys, they are looking for very simple tactics where they can cause mass panic and mass terror and upset the U.S. economy. Now, the weak points they are looking at are major U.S. cities and infrastructure. Whether that is rail, airports, water facilities, hydroelectric trends, anything that will stun the U.S. economy.

They perceive right now that we are under the gun in terms of economic pressures, and that any small push in the wrong direction will cause catastrophe for us. That is their game plan. They are trying to push the United States out of the Middle East. They are trying to create a new world order. You don't do that by killing a few soldiers at Fort Hood. You don't do that by shooting a few soldiers outside an airport in Germany. You do that by creating mass panic in a city like New York or Los Angeles or Detroit. That is what they are gunning for. They may not achieve it, but that is what they are gunning for.

Chairman KING. The time of the gentlelady has expired. The gentleman from South Carolina.

Mr. DUNCAN. Let me thank you for your diligence on keeping our homeland security safe. This is one of the most informative hearings that we have had. I thank the panelists for providing their testimony today. I want to thank Congressman Hamilton for your service to this Nation and also the 9/11 Commission. Interesting, I have been one that has talked about this numerous times, but the 9/11 Commission detailed a lot of different terms that seem to have disappeared from the lexicon of the intelligence agencies, whether FBI, counterterrorism, National intelligence strategy, even the report protecting the force lessons from Fort Hood.

In the 9/11 Commission report, they mentioned jihad 126 times. They mention the Muslim Brotherhood five times. They mention Hamas, Hezbollah, al-Qaeda numerous times, but now that seems to have disappeared. I am very alarmed that our administration is not identifying who our enemy is. I think you have clearly got to identify and focus on the threat to this country, and you guys have very articulately expressed those threats today.

One thing about being a junior Member of this committee, freshman Member, is all the great questions got asked before it gets to me. So what I would like to do is just delve into something that is interesting to me, and that is the threats on our Southern border. I understand that al-Qaeda and Hezbollah and al Shabab have a presence and influence in Latin America, particularly the tri-border region.

So I am going to address this to Mr. Kohlmann. Do you believe the United States may see increasing threats from these groups so close to our Southern border?

Mr. KOHLMANN. It is true that there is a presence below the border of a number of different groups, most prominently Hezbollah and Hamas, not necessarily so much al-Qaeda. I think some of those threats have been blown up, but I think there is a reality that right now we put a tremendous amount of attention on the Northern border. Ever since the days of the Ahmed Ressam, the Algerian who tried crossing over in 1999 in Bellingham, Washington, there has been a lot of focus on the Canadian border. There has been less focus on terrorists crossing the Southern border. Terrorists are aware of this. There are indications of groups like Shabab placing people in Mexico who are able to get folks across the border.

Now, the reality is that a lot of the people they are smuggling across are probably just illegal immigrants, but it is very easy to sneak someone in that group. It is not the most overwhelming issue we have. Really, al-Qaeda would rather recruit someone who is already inside the United States who has a U.S. passport. But these groups are trying to get people in however they can, however it works best. So if they find that they can't recruit someone directly in the United States, I think it is very plausible that they will go for the Southern border.

Mr. DUNCAN. Do you see them working in tandem with the Mexican drug cartel at all? We see some evidence of that, and that is our untalked-about third war possibly.

Mr. KOHLMANN. I think when it comes to groups like Hamas and Hezbollah, there is a potential of individuals doing that. With an ideological group like al-Qaeda, it is much less. Al-Qaeda doesn't seem to like to work with thieves, with drug runners—not publicly anyway. For instance, Shabab al-Mujahideen in Somalia has greatly distanced itself from the pirates, the big problem with piracy in northern Somalia, and they argued simply they don't want to be associated with that, that that is not jihad; that is just thievery.

So as of right now, I don't think you see those connections. The problem is that there are individuals who are in Venezuela and elsewhere who have connections to Hamas and Hezbollah and also connections to the drug-trafficking rings. The issue is can someone like that be marshaled by a terrorist group to serve as an intermediary to get someone into the country? It is possible. But I still think it is relatively far-fetched. The groups really, al-Qaeda, Shabab, they are looking to recruit people who are already within U.S. borders, who already have U.S. passports, who can walk to the middle of Times Square and say, I am a terrorist, and nothing can be done. That is the kind of recruitment.

Mr. DUNCAN. There is a lot of focus on the lone wolf provisions in the PATRIOT Act coming up and sleeper cells. What can we do more—you talked about the marketing, the internet, *Inspire,* and other things targeting those groups. What can we do more than maybe some of the things you alluded to earlier?

Mr. KOHLMANN. I think one of the issues is that the United States has not been engaged in an effective deradicalization campaign, a counterradicalization campaign.

Mr. DUNCAN. The Chairman has.

Mr. KOHLMANN. So far the U.S. Government has been content with simply saying al-Qaeda is bad, al-Qaeda is wrong. But the reality is that there are plenty of voices from within al-Qaeda, from within the Muslim community itself, who will stand forward and will say that these folks are completely on the wrong path, that they are insane, and that the things they are doing are wrong not just from an American perspective, but from a Muslim perspective; from any perspective, from a humanist perspective.

I think it is important that we try to galvanize those resources and engage in an effective deradicalization campaign. So far a lot of the efforts that we have made have fallen on deaf ears, whether it comes through sponsoring television stations and radio stations in Iraq that nobody watches, that nobody listens to, at least not our enemies; or whether it comes to simply broadcasting messages that have no impact.

We also have to realize the effects of negative publicity. Right now we talked about jihadi message forums. What a lot of people don't realize is that even on the top-tier al-Qaeda forums, there is as much argument and nasty back-biting as there is agreement about attacking America. These folks fight with each other on a daily basis. They say nasty things about each other. After the death of bin Laden, a whole bunch of people got their accounts removed from al-Qaeda's top-tier web forums because they dared to "crusade" their claims about the death of bin Laden. These are people expressing sorrow about the death of bin Laden who were removed, kicked off.

I think it is important that the United States take note of the social networking dynamics that are taking place within al-Qaeda and try to exploit those differences. If there are people that don't like Ayman Zawahiri, start pumping information about how terrible Ayman al-Zawahiri is. Trying to sell the United States as a good actor might never work, but explaining the negative things about al-Qaeda and about the people that lead it, you could go on forever. You could write a thousand-page encyclopedia about that.

Chairman KING. The time of the gentleman has expired.

Mr. HAMILTON. Mr. Chairman, excuse me for extending this.

Chairman KING. How can I say no to you?

Mr. HAMILTON. The National Security Preparedness Group now has in draft form a report on preventing violent radicalization in America. It is the most comprehensive thing I have seen—and it is not yet final—dealing with this problem. It makes all kinds of recommendations as to how the government—local, State, National governments—ought to respond to the problem you are raising and which Mr. Kohlmann has talked about.

We consider that a very important report. We will make it available to you as soon as it is ready. It should be ready in the next few months. I think you will find it helpful.

Chairman KING. Thank you.

The gentleman from Massachusetts Mr. Keating.

Mr. KEATING. Thank you, Mr. Chairman.

Just one quick question, because Mr. Kohlmann just touched on this. Social networking. What if many of the very sophisticated devices, deep packet kind of technology, that is involved in—really getting involved in using—potentially using social networking as a weapon, the fact that this kind of technology can detect who is involved and not only filter it, but can actually use that to get information to crack down on people themselves—is it conceivable to you that that kind of sophisticated technology that is available in other countries right now—one of the companies even in the United States that are dealing with this—what is the potential of them gaining access to that kind of technology and using that to crack down on the very people that you and I both agree can serve a very positive role in fighting this?

Mr. KOHLMANN. Well, deep packet inspection rates has a lot of privacy concerns, particularly among groups like EFF; the Electronic Frontier Foundation. I think those fears are grounded except the fact that what you are saying is true is that one of the few ways you can actually find out where someone is located, despite them using proxies or obfuscation techniques, is with deep packet inspection. However, the good news is that that is not the only way. There are other ways, including ways that don't violate U.S. law and don't require us to increasingly impinge upon personal privacy.

One of the good points about this is that al-Qaeda makes mistakes. The folks that create these websites make mistakes. A year and a half ago, my company was able to get the entire database from one of the top-tier al-Qaeda websites, including all their private messages, their IP addresses, everything else like that. We did it without hacking. We did it without deep packet inspection. We did it without infiltration. We just did it using our heads.

So I think as much as having deep packet inspection would be a wonderful tool for law enforcement to have, and it would certainly alleviate a lot of the problems that they are currently facing tracking people, that is not the only way. So if there really are significant privacy concerns, I think the point is just making sure that the Bureau and that other law enforcement agencies and Government agencies have the technological tools to be able to do the job, whether it is deep packet inspection or something else.

I would say right now they are still struggling with this. One of the reasons is because of the legal loopholes that allow foreign law enforcement to use this technique, but not so much for U.S. law enforcement.

Mr. KEATING. Specifically, what about the terrorist organizations themselves being able to obtain that technology?

Mr. KOHLMANN. I think that is relatively far-fetched. I think that is the good news. The good news is that most of the people right now that populate al-Qaeda's social networking web are more interested in blowing themselves up than they are hacking websites. That might change. That probably will change. There are people that are increasingly showing the kind of capabilities you would expect from someone working for the NSA.

I hope that doesn't happen, but I think it is a reminder that the United States needs to be concerned about not just monitoring the communications that are taking place in social networking forums, but making sure our own cybersecurity is up to snuff, because whereas China or Russia may not have hackers who are going to seek to deliberately cause economic catastrophe in the United States, al-Qaeda is a different story. So once they develop those kind of capabilities, it is a serious concern.

Mr. KEATING. Thank you.

Mr. Chairman, I yield back my time.

Chairman KING. The gentleman from Michigan Mr. Walberg is recognized for 5 minutes.

Mr. WALBERG. Thank you, Mr. Chairman, and thank you to the witnesses today for giving us insights that are both encouraging and challenging as well.

In kind-of going back to previous questioning and talking about the impact of trying to grow homegrown terrorists here in the United States, and showing an alternative to the message that they are putting out, I have had a lot of contacts in my district from Assyrians and others concerned with what is going on in Syria, in Libya, and other places. I guess my question would be what impact, if there is—what impact could our actions or inactions in Libya or Syria have in growing al-Qaeda efforts in recruitment of terrorists and terrorist action against the United States?

Chairman KING. If I can just interject. I understand Chairman Hamilton has to leave at 11:45. Whenever you feel you have to leave. Thank you very much for your testimony.

Mr. HAMILTON. Thank you very much, Mr. Chairman. I appreciate that. I will leave to my colleagues to answer these simple questions that have been asked.

Mr. WALBERG. That is as simple as I can be, I guess.

Mr. BERGEN. I just don't think that is really a relevant question right now for the discussion we are having. Somehow the war actions in Libya—and Evan can correct me if I am wrong on this issue—I don't think are something that is really of great interest to the jihadist community, partly because they know very well that the whole point of their exercise was to overthrow these dictators like Qadhafi. That was the point of these groups. So it would be very dissonant for them to say, well, now America is involved in actually producing the very thing that we tried to do in the first place. So they are kind of ignoring it.

One of the things that was very interesting to me is bin Laden really never replied to the Arab Spring because what was he going to say; at last it was happening. Belatedly we have a minor tape from him. But he was commenting on even the most minor news events before his death. This enormous seismic shift in the Middle East he didn't really acknowledge publicly before his death. So I think that this is not going to be a problem.

But on the issue of the Muslim American community, we are never going to be able to take down these jihadi websites. The internet doesn't work like that. What the Chairman and the Members of the committee and, I think, Lee Hamilton and his group, what we need to be thinking about with the Muslim American community is counternarratives. There are plenty of people in the Muslim community that want to get out there and put out a counternarrative to bin Laden and others. One of the problems they face is they are not necessarily that computer literate. They don't understand Google bombing or these kinds of issues, ways to make their messages more attractive.

So that is the way forward. It is not taking down objectionable websites. They are only going to pop up again. It is about creating a counternarrative. At the end of the day, that is the Muslim American community, not the U.S. Government. But that is the way forward.

Mr. KOHLMANN. I think I agree with Peter. I would just say this. It is not clear exactly what is going to fall out of Libya, but there are indications that al-Qaeda supporters and its leadership are getting very frustrated by the fact that the Libyan rebels seem more intent upon courting crusader support than they are al-Qaeda support.

A few months ago a group of foreign fighters from Egypt went to Libya, and they later wrote about their experiences. They showed up, and what they found was: (A) Chaos; (B) as soon as they identified who they were, the Libyan rebels said, we don't want you here, go away. Then they basically went out to the front anyway, and they discovered it was chaos there, too. They came back and said, these guys don't know what they are doing, they don't like us, and they are not fighting under a banner of Islam. It was deeply demoralizing for them.

I think if you read between the lines in the last couple of speeches that have been given by Ayman al-Zawahiri and other senior al-Qaeda leaders, you do kind of hear desperation in their voice, saying to the Libyans, don't work with NATO, don't work with NATO. It is wrong. It is wrong. It is wrong.

Mr. WALBERG. Is there a similar response in Syria as well?

Mr. KOHLMANN. Syria, unfortunately, is a much different picture. I think part of the problem is that it is not clear in Syria what exactly Syrian demonstrators want. Some want democracy, that is for sure. But the Syrians are not necessarily being mobilized and have the same concerns as the Libyans do. I think that is part of the issue.

One of the major concerns with Syria is that the Muslim Brotherhood branch in Syria is far more conservative and I think you can say far more radical than in other States, particularly in Egypt. The Syrian Muslim Brotherhood, numerous members have joined al-Qaeda. The Syrian Muslim Brotherhood is obviously 100 percent opposed to the existence of the State of Israel. It is 100 percent opposed to the idea of peace with the Israelis. If you have the Brotherhood start influencing major impact on Syrian policy, I think as a starting point you can say forget about it to Middle East peace.

I think this is really what we are talking about. Syria is in a different location. It is far more strategically located. The political dynamics there are far more complicated than Libya. I don't think you are going to see John McCain visiting Syria anytime soon. Also, you have the additional factor of Iran. Libya, Muammar Qadhafi really doesn't have any allies to speak of other than Hugo Chavez. Right. Syria has Iran. Though Iran, I think, is worried about what it is seeing there right now, the Iranians, I think, will back Bashar al-Assad to the hilt.

Chairman KING. The time of the gentleman has expired.

The gentleman from Texas, Mr. Green.

Mr. GREEN. Thank you, Mr. Chairman. I thank you and the Ranking Member for allowing me to continue to interlope. I thank you also for conducting and having this hearing today.

I would like to say to the panelists as sort of a predicate for my eventual question, I believe in America, and I believe that if the world did not have the United States of America, we would have to create it. It may not be the glue that holds the world together; I do believe, however, that it is an indispensable ingredient in that glue that holds the world together.

I am finding more and more that I am hearing the notion that we are interlopers; that we should not concern ourselves with Hezbollah and Nasrallah in Lebanon. We should not concern ourselves with the Muslim Brotherhood in Syria and in Egypt. We should not concern ourselves with Hamas in Palestine. We should not concern ourselves with the vituperative comments of Mahmoud Ahmadinejad with reference to what he thinks of another country and how he doesn't see the existence of that country.

This notion that we should remove our assets, bring our resources home, seems to be gaining some degree of credibility. I would ask each of you to just explain whether this would bring about the peace within that some seem to think is available to us if we would but only withdraw our assets.

I will start with Ms. Townsend, please. Thank you.

Ms. TOWNSEND. Thank you, Congressman.

The most recent, let me say historical, example was we waited far too long to exert our leadership in Afghanistan, and look what happened. It was an ungoverned space that al-Qaeda used to plan and to train to attack the United States on September 11, but before that. We can't abrogate our sense of leadership without jeopardizing our own security. That does not mean that we need to lead alone. It does not mean that we don't have allies and build coalitions, all of which is right and appropriate. But we are going to have to lead because it is—there has been a discussion now about Syria and Hezbollah. Hezbollah remains an incredibly strong threat to us because they are a client of Iran's, and they are a destabilizing force not only in Syria, but throughout the Middle East and to the peace and security of Israel.

I agree with you wholeheartedly that we need to continue to engage and not—my fear is that as we begin to engage less, we engage more rhetorically and are unwilling to put ourselves at risk. I think it is incredibly important. If we care about the outcome in Libya, we need to more than just answer rhetorically, and we need to be willing to put our assets against a real and very credible problem there.

Chairman KING. If the witnesses can keep their answer to 1 minute.

Mr. BERGEN. I want to take an opportunity about Afghanistan, because obviously many Members of the committee are going to have to think about this pretty carefully. We are spending $118 billion there.

First of all, 68 percent of Afghans have a favorable view of international forces. This is an astonishing number for a Muslim country. That is a BBC poll taken in December.

Second, we are not there because of al-Qaeda; we are there because every Islamic terrorist or insurgent group in the world was headquartered or based there before 9/11, and they have migrated across the border to Pakistan, where they are now being guests of the Pakistani Taliban.

Third, when we overthrow a government, we have somewhat of a responsibility, I think, and I think many others would share this, to kind of leave the place in a somewhat stable condition.

Fourth, the most likely place in the world for a nuclear war is between Pakistan and India. An unstable Afghanistan leads to an unstable Pakistan. We have already seen that.

Fifth, the Taliban are the Taliban. We have seen what they have done just recently in Pakistan. This is not a bunch of Henry Kissingers in waiting. You know who they are. Just to amplify something that Fran just said, we have already run this experiment twice before in Afghanistan. We closed our embassy in 1989, zeroed out aid in the 1990s, and we did it again in 2002. We got what we paid for. We did it on the cheap. So we were attacked from Afghanistan, as you know.

So we need to be very careful about how we are going to pull out obviously over time. The Afghans were freaking out at the idea we were leaving this year in July, as we said, or seemed to say. So we need to think very carefully about how we manage that withdrawal over time.

Mr. KOHLMANN. I wish I could say that I thought that U.S. forces could be withdrawn from Afghanistan by and large and that everything would be peachy, but I don't think that is the reality. As much as I wish U.S. forces could come home right away, I do remember what it was like before 9/11, meeting with folks at the NSC at the White House, talking about the issue of Afghanistan as a sanctuary, and their frustration with the fact that the U.S. Government was doing nothing about it.

So whenever I think about withdrawing, I think back to those days and back to the idea that the last thing we need right now is for Afghanistan to once again become a sanctuary for al-Qaeda after all of the effort we put in to try to prevent it from becoming so.

Chairman KING. The time of the gentleman has expired.

The former attorney general of California, Mr. Lungren.

Mr. LUNGREN. Thank you very much, Mr. Chairman. I am sorry to the panelists that I had to leave for a while to Chair another committee, so I hope I am not repeating what has been asked of you before.

First of all, just a comment. We talked about the necessity for a deradicalization program, a counterradicalization program. In order for us to get that support for such a program, we have to admit there is radicalization going on. The Chairman held a hearing on that, and the message that we thought we were going to get out about the radicalization of youth in the Muslim communities in America, with testimony by a parent and an uncle of two that had been so radicalized, was lost in the coverage, and, frankly, the Chairman was attacked because we dared to deal with the issue. So I appreciate the fact you recognize that we have to do something about a deep radicalization or counterradicalization program, but first you have to assume there is a radicalization by putting that on the record.

Second, I would like to ask the three of you this: We started out this hearing by talking about the treasure trove of intelligence that we got from the successful mission executed against Osama bin Laden. I was asked this question when I was home recently at a town hall meeting. They said, what possible benefit was given to us by our releasing the fact that we had gotten this treasure trove of intelligence; and, second, by giving out some parts of that intelligence; and third, by revealing the manner and means by which we obtained the intelligence when we executed the mission?

Frankly, I was at a loss to try and answer that with my constituents. My only answer was perhaps there was a judgment that this would put them on notice that we were after them. But at the same time, that is certainly not what we did during World War II and every other thing. We thought the utilization of intelligence was enhanced by the fact that the enemy didn't know we had it. Could the three of you have help me in that regard?

Chairman KING. I know Ms. Townsend is supposed to leave at noon. We should be finished with the hearing by about 12:05.

Ms. TOWNSEND. Thank you, Chairman. I am good. Thanks.

Let me say, you mentioned the radicalization issue. Quickly, this is a fact. Quite frankly, whether or not there is radicalization of youth here in the United States is not a political issue open to debate. So people just need to suck up and get over that. It is a fact. It is happening. We have credible instances of it. So it should not be an issue of debate.

On the treasure trove, I will say to you, having served in the White House, when you have a successful disruption, I can tell you that I have suffered under the sort of excruciating pressure from the press to get some details out to inform the American people. You do want, because it goes to the complacency issue. If you can explain to the American people a successful disruption, you can get their support for further operations. So there is this balance.

Let me quickly add that releasing the fact that there was a trove, the details of the operation, and the manner and means in which it was executed are terribly harmful. I feel that releasing those details—we are going to have to have future operations, and we are going to have to put men and women in harm's way. Releasing those details, we know that al-Qaeda monitors what we call open-source material, news reports. We found them in the caves of Afghanistan. So have no doubt that the details that we release will be used against men and women in future operations. So, on balance, I would not have released the level of detail that was released.

Mr. LUNGREN. Mr. Bergen.

Mr. BERGEN. I think there is a certain utility in letting al-Qaeda know that we have found the Rosetta Stone, for the following reason. They are in a kind of Catch-22. They can communicate with each other and, therefore, open themselves to being detected, or not communicate forever, in which case they are sort of out of business.

What did we really release in terms of actual details of the information trove? I think we said that the plans were in New York, and Washington, and Chicago, and Los Angeles. Well, I think we knew that.

So I think there is—Fran has explained, as she was really there for many, many years, what the pressures are. Let us see what comes out of this. But there might be a certain utility in letting al-Qaeda know this.

Mr. LUNGREN. Mr. Kohlmann.

Mr. KOHLMANN. I appreciate the idea of sending a chilled fear down al-Qaeda's spine, and I understand that potentially this also could be simply a way of trying to get al-Qaeda operatives to start moving around out of fear and see where people are moving to, who is moving. There was a convoy attacked in the last few days. Mullah Omar. Perhaps he was afraid that his hiding place had been discovered, and he decided to high-tail it.

So I understand that there is a utility to this, but I, too, recognize the fact that al-Qaeda has a dramatic interest in open-source intelligence. AQAP has an entire section of their *Inspire* magazine dedicated to open-source intelligence. They are parsing through every single statement put out by the White House, they are parsing through every single news conference. They are watching very carefully for every detail they can glean, and they will use it against us. They have in the past, and they will in the future. That is a concern.

I think there were certain things that probably could have been stated about the raid, but some things that were released I am not sure provide any benefit. The releasing of the videos of bin Laden, I think, would have been a tremendously amount more effective had there been sound, because right now all we have are the description of U.S. officials saying, well, he is mumbling here. Well, that is not what we are seeing. When we see the video of bin Laden wrapped in a shawl watching TV, it is 5 seconds long. There is no context to it.

So I think some of this information was released with the right intent, but I am not sure the execution was there.

Chairman KING. The time of the gentleman has expired.

The gentleman from Illinois, Mr. Walsh.

Mr. WALSH. Thank you, Mr. Chairman. It has been a long morning, so let us close.

Ms. Townsend, you have given me my best takeaway line of the hearing: It is a fact, radicalization here at home. Just your overview thoughts on this topic.

It is a fact, but we know politically it is also a debate in this country. Why is it still a debate? Fort Hood, you referenced that we saw warning signs. Why weren't they heeded, and what needs to be done to make sure they are heeded again? It is a fact, but why doesn't the whole country seem to understand that?

Ms. TOWNSEND. I will take a stab at this. I think part of it is it is a fact. If you can point to cases and examples, the conversation tends to stay reasonably rational, in my experience.

So you point to Nidal Hasan. There is no question he was an American soldier who was radicalized, and that is part of a pattern that we know of Anwar al-Awlaki. But I think we also have to acknowledge that there are Muslim Americans, while they don't often wish to be named publicly, who have cooperated with law enforcement agencies like the FBI, like the Department of Homeland Security. These aren't either/or issues. Both facts happen to be true. There are many Muslim Americans who abhor al-Qaeda, who abhor the ideals and ideologue of al-Qaeda, wish to be helpful. This is not a single "ummah" of the Muslim world who subscribe to this.

But to Congressman Lungren's point, until people accept the fact of radicalization of American youth, we can't effectively combat it. So what we need to do is, frankly, the best way to fight it is this whole notion of a counternarrative. We need to employ, encourage, and recruit Muslim Americans to participate in that counternarrative.

Mr. BERGEN. Fran used the helpful phrase "it is not an either/or." I think there is another either/or which is part of this, which is, as I mentioned earlier, 17 Americans have been killed in jihadist American attacks since 9/11. In the same time, 73 Americans were killed in hate crimes, according to the FBI, which have different motivations. So jihadist terrorism is obviously a National security problem of the United States, but there are other problems. It is not the only one.

So I think part of the controversy around the hearing, Mr. Chairman, was the idea that this was the only or the most important problem. I think the Muslim American community felt there were other issues that were important as well.

Chairman KING. If I can just address that. Obviously it is the most important homeland security issue. There are other issues in the Judiciary Committee and other committees, but the Department of Homeland Security was set up to counter the attacks of September 11. Other issues we have had before, and they are cer-

81

tainly appropriate for other committees to discuss, but I felt this
issue in particular was essential for this committee.

Mr. WALSH. Just to leapfrog on that for a second, it is my fear
that that sensitive attitude we might have might continue us down
this path—and, Mr. Kohlmann, you can close this whole thing—
with us not heeding the warning signs of another potential Fort
Hood because we are afraid of whatever.

Mr. KOHLMANN. I feel tremendous sympathy for the Muslim community in this country and around the world. I understand that
the vast majority of Muslims have no interest in terrorism or al-
Qaeda. I understand why they are sensitive about this. It is very
difficult when it seems like your faith is under attack, especially
in the context of Koran burnings and the whole thing about the
Ground Zero mosque. It is understandable that people get sensitive
about this.

I agree with Fran. I don't think it is a question, it is not a political question. There is radicalization going on. I think it is in the
interests of the Muslim community above all else to be at the forefront of making sure that we deal with this problem because it is
their children who are being recruited to go off and join foreign terrorist organizations. It is their children who are watching videos of
people being beheaded on the internet and think that is a good
thing. It is not their fault, but it is an issue that needs to be addressed. I think one thing that Muslims should understand is that
this is not just an attack on Islam, it is not an attack on mosques.

In my written testimony I describe an individual who was
radicalized inside this country in Pennsylvania, who never at-
tended a mosque, who never went to an Islamic center, who wasn't
really a Muslim.

Again, I understand their sensitivity, but this is not about them.
It is about terrorism, it is about terrorists, and it is about how all
Americans can try to prevent radicalization and people being
pushed to join extremist causes.

Mr. WALSH. Thank you. Go get lunch.

Thank you, Mr. Chairman.

Chairman KING. Thank you, Mr. Walsh.

First of all, let me thank all the witnesses. This has been a great,
great panel, great hearing, and speaking for the Ranking Member,
it was extremely illuminating and informative.

Members of the committee may have additional questions for the
witnesses. I will ask you to respond to them in writing. The record
will be kept open for 10 days.

Without objection, the committee stands adjourned.

[Whereupon, at 12:05 p.m., the committee was adjourned.]

○